Family Matters

Family Matters:
The Influence of the Family in Career Decision Making

By

Robert C. Chope, Ph.D.

San Francisco State University

© 2006 by Pro-Ed, Inc.
8700 Shoal Creek Blvd.
Austin, TX 78757-6897
800/897-3202   Fax 800/397-7633
www.proedinc.com

ISBN 1-4164-0063-x

This book was developed and produced by CAPS Press, formerly
associated with ERIC/CASS, and creator of many titles for the
counseling, assessment, and educational fields. In 2004, CAPS Press
became an independent imprint of PRO-ED, Inc.

Printed in the United States of America

1   2   3   4   5   6   7   8   9   10   08   07   06   05   04

Dedication

This book is dedicated to my siblings and those of my partner, Roberta Ann Johnson, Ph.D.

Carol Ann Austin
Nikki Feit
Alan Johnson
Suellen Johnson
William A. Chope

You can't imagine how useful you were in preparing this work. You've given me a lifetime of ideas.

Table of Contents

Dedication .... *v*

Foreword .... *ix*

Preface .... *xi*

Chapter 1
  Why Should Career Counselors Even Bother with the Family? *1*

Chapter 2
  An Update on Current Research *23*

Chapter 3
  Cultural Diversity and Family Influence *41*

Chapter 4
  How to Gather Data to Assess Family Influence *63*

Chapter 5
  The Nature of Decision Making *89*

Chapter 6
  Out of the Home and into the Classroom *113*

Chapter 7
  Looking to the Future *135*

References *155*

Foreword

Long forewords are like long introductions for speakers – they don't really help poor speakers and they are superfluous for good speakers. Hence, this foreword for a new author to the former ERIC/CASS family of authors (now CAPS Press, in partnership with PRO-ED, Inc.) can be succinct. First off, Bob Chope is a writer whose prose is both knowledge based and interesting to read. Novices and experts alike find his writing compelling. We are delighted to have him join our family of authors both because he writes so well and because he addresses topics we believe to be important to the field of counseling.

In this first monograph with us, *Family Matters: The Influence of the Family in Career Decision Making,* Bob Chope has met our four-fold test for writing with flying colors. First, he demonstrates a thorough knowledge of the subject gained from both personal experience as well as familiarity with the research and literature in the field. Second, his writing style draws readers in to the extent that they can't put the book down. Third, the book is chock-full of exercises and activities which provide instant opportunities for readers to experience first hand his key points. Fourth, he explores and probes new topics and ideas before they become commonplace. Hence, his writing is of interest to and used by a broad array of readers, including researchers, educators, practitioners, and anyone with interest in the field.

All of the above make him like a favorite author whose new works will be ones readers eagerly await. I am convinced that, like our entire staff, Bob Chope will become a must-read author whenever he produces a new work.

We will keep you informed. I know you will want to read his next new work after you have the satisfaction of reading this one.

Garry R. Walz, Ph.D., CEO
CAPS Press, LLC

Preface

This book represents my continuing effort to intertwine some of the personal issues that career counselors must address. After all, it is impossible to treat career issues in a vacuum even though much of the training of the career practitioner avoids personal issues. This has been well documented in the literature

The goal of the book is to explore career decision making and its roots in the family of origin. While "families of creation," i.e., those which are created through marriage or partnerships, also affect a person's career decisions, a discussion of their influences is beyond the scope of this book. In both areas there is an unfortunate paucity of research and there is certainly room for consideration of the family of creation in career decision making in a future monograph. Issues of attitudes toward two career or two job families, stay-at-home moms, career mommy tracks, and the difficulties of returning to work after child rearing represent some of these issues.

Men and women often take on different roles and change their career aspirations after creating a life together or making the decision to raise children. The lack of recognition for excellent child rearing, keeping a relationship intact, or volunteering for important social causes is a loss that is not completely compensated for by the applause that people receive at work.

While the book may have a few examples of family of creation issues, these are here only because they illustrate a point that is better exemplified with the present case material or it is a case that I have had some experience with and decided to share.

The book is intended as a "crossover" book so that it is written in a style that will be useful for counselor educators and career counselors as well as for general readers who are interested in why they feel as they do about their job or why they decided to pursue the career that they did.

For many, the process of career selection often takes place in a way that appears on its face to be unconscious. Yet, later in life, upon reflection, people often find that the reasons for their career choices are based upon a combination of genetic constitution, family history, cultural context, educational and career family values, and other more specific variables like the presence of a war, or good luck, or a catastrophic mishap.

In addition to providing a "because" to answer the "why" questions people have about their careers, the book should also be useful to those people who are raising children to explore what can be done to assist in the career decision making and educational planning process.

The book is replete with case examples as well as career stories that have been drawn from my 25 years of career counseling practice along with news stories in the popular press.

I want to thank a number of people who have been involved in the project from the onset. As always and with each of my monographs, I am forever indebted to my partner, Roberta Ann Johnson, Ph.D., Professor of Politics at the University of San Francisco. There has never been an editor who could be at once so loving and kind, thoughtful, creative, and nudgingly critical. While we have very different styles, her stamp of approval rests throughout the text. I also want to thank two of my former students at San Francisco State University, Rachel Klein and Malia Kawaguchi, for their willingness to read the text and offer creative comments. In my many years of teaching, they represent the finest of what we have to offer in the Career Counseling program. Both are extraordinarily gifted writers and will undoubtedly make their own substantial contributions in the years to come.

Finally, great appreciation is extended to Garry R. Walz, Ph.D., for his suggestion of the project and continuing enthusiasm. Garry remains a colleague and mentor to untold numbers of professionals, and I am delighted to be in the fold with so many distinguished others.

San Francisco, CA

Chapter 1

Why Should Career Counselors Even Bother with the Family?

"To find out what one is fitted to do, and to secure an opportunity to do it, is the key to happiness."
John Dewey

Career stories about family influence on career decision making set the stage for the chapter and book. New career theories with a contextual focus are briefly described to demonstrate how family historical information can be used to help people in their career planning. Reasons for why family influence is more important now than ever before are discussed along with suggestions for expanding the focus of career counseling training.

Increasing the Saliency of the Family

Why should a career counselor bother to be interested in a client's family of origin? In fact, why should anybody, including job seekers and students making career and life plans, care about whether their families influenced them in the past or are influencing them now? In the pages to follow, the answers to these questions will become clear.

This book focuses upon a neglected, often ignored issue in career decision making: how the family of origin affects the process of deciding upon a career path. This first chapter will provide some anecdotal evidence and set the stage for demonstrating how important family bias about career choice can be.

Family influence shouldn't be trivialized or appear as a mere add-on to a career counselor's check list. Counselors need to develop approaches that deepen the entire career planning process in a systematic way. They should consider spending less energy on crystallizing outcomes of the career counseling process and more on facilitating greater degrees of exploration by their clients. Through a refocusing of their purpose, career counselors, along with advisors and coaches, can begin to experience how family background, history, mobility, support, conflicts, nurturing, exposure to new ideas or protection from them affect the process of determining what clients hope to do with the rest of their lives. Using a more holistic approach, and with appropriate data gathering, interventions, guidance, and support from career counselors, career clients can learn to engage family members as partners in a collaborative career planning process. Both counselors and their clients can begin to envision the issues that must be addressed as life issues, not simply career issues. And as I've pointed out elsewhere (Chope, 2001b), maybe clients shouldn't do all of their work alone. Bringing in family members to help could be wonderfully beneficial to the career decision making process.

Examples are Everywhere

It doesn't take much searching, really, to find examples of the influence of the family on career planning. The career coach Mary Jacobsen (2000) has written how the dreams of parents and caregivers, even their unattained dreams, shape the career choices of their offspring. She opines that what the family hands down is a "vision of human life—what it means to be a good person: what constitutes success or failure; what our responsibilities are to ourselves and others" (p. 66).

But there are also many cases in which the vision, judgments, and wishes of parents are vastly different from those of their children. Viewing the world through strikingly different lenses can be disenchanting. We all want to matter to somebody and the people whom we believe we matter to first are our parents. So it hurts, with ravages of guilt, when we feel that we've disappointed them in some way. Wendy Wasserstein's experience illustrates this point. When she won the Pulitzer Prize for *The Heidi Chronicles*, her mother candidly shrieked that she wished that she were celebrating Wendy's wedding instead (Aron, 2003). Obviously, comments like that, especially at the celebration of a career high point, can make anyone feel that no matter the accomplishment, if it's not consistent with the family agenda, it doesn't count. Our first task is to hurdle the family acceptability threshold.

Family history and unfortunate events can also affect how people contemplate their futures. Norm Amundson (1998) describes a man whose father was dreadfully unsuccessful and faced bankruptcy when he endeavored to form a new business (p. 69). The son didn't want to relive his father's troubling anxiety, so he chose work that had the components of security, teaching. Problem was, then as now, changing economic times can foster insecurity in the job market even in the most potentially secure careers. Amundson comments that this young man was traumatized by the thought of losing his job. And to add insult to the circumstance, he realized, through counseling, that he didn't care for teaching after all! Clearly, background information like this about the family is necessary for a counselor to understand why a particular client finds risk taking so aversive that he seeks secure employment situations above consideration of personal career preferences.

Jacobsen, Wasserstein, and Amundson can certainly whet our appetite for more details and illustrations as we reposition the role of the family in the decision making process. But, in order to explore family influence in a meaningful way, we ought to consider a few more examples in greater detail. These are drawn from my own clinical practice or from my meanderings through the popular and academic presses. They give fitting prototypes that can serve to point out how the often forgotten variable of family is very much in operation, but usually not consciously considered in the career decision making process.

The readers are invited to try to find themselves in one or more of the examples. Although the stories have different outcomes and feature a variety of family influences and interventions, they all illustrate the power of the family on career decisions. Let's begin with two people whose career choices were programmed by their family's traditions and expectations.

Clients' Choices Programmed by the Family and Tradition

David. David was a tortured and miserably unhappy urologist. He frequently moaned to his colleagues that he felt like he was suffocating in his job. So, with more than a little prodding from his friends and mentors, he made an appointment to consult with a private career counselor. Visiting with his counselor, or career doctor as he called him, he ruminated about the easily available opportunities he had earlier in life. In a quietly depressed tone, he focused mostly upon the ones he chose not to pursue or let get away. Musician, rock star, songwriter, entrepreneur, chief executive, screen writer, and film critic had all crossed his mind over the years.

Musician came up most frequently. "I could have played lead guitar in a great rock band," he mused, adding, "but, I also have a keen eye and mind for business. And I don't really like science. So why am I a doctor? I had such potential for so many challenges and now it feels wasted." He openly regretted not attending business school like so many of his classmates from college. Instead, with his good grades and superlative Medical College Admissions Test (MCAT) scores he pursued medical education, following in the footpaths of his father and grandfather.

By all standards of professional success, David had performed admirably. So why was he so unhappy, seeking out a career counselor to listen to him remonstrate at length about doctoring? It took a while for him to finally confess, sadly, that his parents, especially his father, never wanted to discuss any other career except being a doctor. Turns out, through counseling David realized he had discarded all other choices. That's quite a contrast to his original belief that he made the decision to be a doctor. "The pressure on me was enormous. Like the day I was born, my father said, 'Well, another generation of doctors. It can't get better than this.'"

To his father, medical school and a lifetime of clinical practice serving others had no higher calling. Yet, David remembered ironically that his father never seemed all that happy with his practice, and the work most assuredly interfered with his having any opportunity to spend quality time with the family. David recalled as a youngster waiting in the car, time after time, to travel to a vacation destination while his father returned emergency phone calls from his patients. Reflecting on his own life trek he said, "It's not like I wanted to be a doctor or had any passion for it. And now all of my friends from college who went on to business school have been financially successful. And what's worse, they all seem to be very happy. I can't imagine doing this doctoring for the rest of my life. I can't imagine being this unhappy. What's worse, with managed care affecting my life the way it does, I don't have much income to show for my efforts. And future earnings don't look great either."

Before coming to counseling, David's career seemed like it was headed for an ash heap and morose decay. His story is hardly uncommon. Career counselors have heard similarly woeful tales, rife with such dilemmas, before. To be sure, contextual variables like family of origin, intimate relationships, friendships, culture, social and economic status, the job market and hot new careers in dot coms and nanotechnology all contribute to the package of possibilities that people use to fantasize about their future. As much as counselors and the lay public can take these contextual variables for granted, for decades there has been only a passing interest among career professionals in how the family of origin affects the career decision making process.

Yet there's a vast potential garden of material even for those who study career decision making for a living; and some career experts are beginning to expend more effort in understanding family influence as they reflect upon their own career choices. Let's look at another example that demonstrates strong family influence.

Rachel Naomi Remen. A few years ago healing artist, physician, and author Dr. Rachel Naomi Remen (1996) described the pervasive influence of her grandfather on her own career choice. Her personal and career related profile described a childhood overtaken by a world of medicine. In two generations of her family, she wrote, there are three nurses and nine physicians. As a young child she pondered that, "You became an adult and a doctor as part of the same process." With what appears to be some unforgotten frustration, she recalls she was the only premed student in kindergarten. When her grandfather, an orthodox rabbi, died, he left her the resources to attend medical school; she was seven at the reading of the will. Still, with the literary humor aside, Rachel admits that the weight of her "family expectations began to grow heavy."

In both of these illustrations, David and Rachel, the role of generational family persuasion is enormous. Both attended medical school, despite their other interests. Rachel's undergraduate degree was in philosophy and she secretly found science to be "colorless and cold." And both felt the pressure of tradition from individuals living and dead. But unlike David, Rachel was able to develop a career path more her own, after medical school. Interestingly, Rachel went on to become a well established author, more like the rabbi that she recalls she wanted to be when she was 12.

While expectation may, indeed, have a negative impact on the career decision making process, there are also examples where family can have an overwhelmingly positive impact. The following examples portray the role of family members as persistent supporters.

Family Members as Understanding Interveners

Zac, the Reluctant Firefighter. Zac Unger is a firefighter who resides and works in Oakland, California. A self-titled "nice Jewish boy," he came from a family of intellectuals who expected substantial accomplishments. Like David described earlier, Zac's father is a physician, a psychiatrist, while his late grandfather was a cardiologist. His mother is a community college professor and her parents were both teachers.

As chronicled by Annie Nakao (2004), Zac took an uncommon path to becoming a member of the Oakland Fire Department's Fire Station 12. He attended private preparatory schools in Oakland and the small, but highly competitive and prestigious Deep Springs College, a two-year program in California's high desert that combines strenuous outdoor activity with highly intellectual teaching and philosophical discussions. Thereafter, he matriculated at Brown University, graduating in 1996 with an environmental sciences degree. For the next two years he took on a series of physically demanding activities with plans to be involved in a career in some area of wildlife management. Forest ranger or "fish and game man" were certainly possibilities as Nakao points out. But Zac was actually lost with regard to a career development plan that would fit in with his own and his family's expectations. He drifted from job to job failing to confront the dilemma of following his heart into more physically demanding pursuits, or fulfilling his legacy of impacting the world through social contributions.

Zac's mother, on the other hand, was the wife of a doctor and not the daughter of one. Hoping to help her son, she noticed an announcement in her neighborhood for a job as a firefighter in Oakland. She knew that Zac had more of a passion for physical activity than for wildlife; even as a little boy he enjoyed physical challenges. Perhaps, she thought, being a firefighter might be invigorating and fun for her son. Zac, on the other hand, couldn't see how this kind of paramilitary work with its uniforms and all would fit into a meaningful life plan. Still, his mother picked up an application and with her encouragement, he filled it out. Meanwhile, Zac enrolled in graduate school at UC-Berkeley. In 1998, he was accepted into the Oakland Fire Academy and, with family support, became a firefighter.

The family role in this circumstance, especially the mother's, is a most interesting one. Who knows what she really thought of her son's career choice, but her definition of him as an adventurer and a bright, rugged individual was hardly fleeting. She undoubtedly thought that any job with stability was better than no job at all, so she encouraged him to apply as a firefighter and let the chips fall where they may. Unquestionably, his career up to that point lacked direction.

To be sure, Zac's mom knew about college teaching. College professorships, even at the California Community College level, are highly competitive and demanding. To her credit, she didn't push Zac to partake of continued graduate studies that would lead to a career in college teaching because she probably figured that he would have a difficult time obtaining a tenure track position anyway. Fortunately, there wasn't a lot of pressure on him to become a physician either.

There's a delightful finale to the story, however. What makes this tale so promising is that after Zac became a firefighter, he also became a writer. The firefighting job, with its odd mix of days on and days off lends itself to the opportunity for some to pursue other endeavors. Many firefighters have second income streams. I've consulted with a few who were roofers, lawyers, teachers, and painters.

Zac published his first book on firefighting, *Working Fire* (Unger, 2004), an insightful book that explores the human characteristics that make up the careers of firefighters. His career has allowed him to satisfy his physical activity needs and his creative urges. Clearly he would never have pursued becoming a firefighter had he not received practical support from his mother and a lack of pressure from his physician father.

Jack London. We can add to this section of material by recounting another Oakland, California writer, the namesake of the city square, Jack London. As reported by Tyche Hendricks (2003), Jack London, unlike Zac, had a checkered childhood, but like Zac he too was a rugged individual who didn't seem to rally around any particular career pursuit. He had to work out of his home at an early age to assist his widowed mother, and by the age of 15, was a fisherman and somewhat Machiavellian "oyster bed robber." He had a purportedly "uneven" early public education experience. And interestingly, he became somewhat of a political radical and socialist. Hendricks writes that he was recognized for his cracker barrel philosophizing against "injustice and poverty." Moreover, he was an avid reader and spent many long hours in local libraries, devouring whatever he could.

When he was 21, Jack decided to break away and head north in order to participate in the Klondike gold rush of 1897. He failed miserably as a gold digger and returned home, broke, after 16 months. But from that experience, he began to pen yarns about his compelling travels.

Oakland at the turn of the century was known for its unforgiving environment; there weren't many opportunities for mounting a career campaign. Jack was frustrated with his wobbly start establishing himself independently either at home or away, so he eventually decided to apply for work in the local post office. Meanwhile, his mother quietly began to read through his memoirs and short stories from the Klondike experience and became aware that her son had the gift to be a top flight writer. She discouraged him from joining the post office and gave him whatever support she could to encourage him to continue his writing. So, he organized and edited his papers from the gold rush and started submitting them for publication.

It wasn't long before London was a contributor to the *Atlantic Monthly* and in 1900 the publisher Houghton-Mifflin put out his first collection of short stories. By 1903, he was thought to be the wealthiest writer in America, according to Hendricks.

These two examples illustrate how family members can help with career suggestions based upon their perceptions of the individual interests, needs, skills, personal characteristics, and perseverance of their children. The communications by these two mothers were facilitative, direct, and presumably powerful.

However compelling the influence of the family is in career decision making, it often goes undetected unless pointed out by others. As a counselor, I'm struck by how many individuals are completely insensitive to the direct influences of their families. Most sense that their parents "just wanted them to be happy." Jack London may not have noticed the subtle but critical role his mother played in his quest to become a writer. Zac didn't easily credit his mother for influencing him and was probably undiscerning of her gentle encouragement until later reflection.

However, unlike the experiences of Zac and Jack London, sometimes the communication to a family member from a parent or relative is incomplete or a trifle too vague and the family member can't really take advantage of it. That situation is illustrated in the distinguished career and behavioral psychologist John Krumboltz's recollections of his father and how he affected his thoughts about a future career.

Incomplete Communication From the Family

John Krumboltz. John Krumboltz shared information about his own career development when he won the American Psychological Association Award for Distinguished Professional Contribution to Knowledge (APA, 2002). His father was an attorney and, according to Krumboltz, when his father brought work home from the office like abstracts of ownership records of land parcels, it looked like "gibberish to his ten year old mind." He remembered, somewhat excitedly, that he considered any number of occupations, perhaps even becoming a musician or a baseball player. And even though he'd considered becoming a lawyer like his dad, he decided to "scratch lawyer from his list of future occupations" (p. 928).

In the midst of this meditative personal speculation on his career, Krumboltz offers an approach that parents, and indeed counselors, might consider useful if they are to become more helpful and direct in the decision making or career planning process. Krumboltz wonders whether or not he would have thought differently about becoming a lawyer if his father had been more active in drawing him into the lawyering process. He speculates aloud about what might have been the consequence had he, in his youth, actually been able to help his father with his legal work? Krumboltz thought that he would have been "thrilled to have helped his father. He would have learned one of the tasks that lawyers perform. He would have felt efficacious in performing that task and might have considered a future career as a lawyer" (p. 928).

So in his musing, Krumboltz creates an exquisite template for parents to use to assist their children in an open, friendly, and positive way with the career decision making process. Parents should give their children more complete information about their own careers, even bidding them to help with a work related problem. Elementary and secondary school counselors can learn from this recollection and remind parents to show their children their work and let them envision what it might be like to actually be employed in the jobs of their parents or caregivers. These pivotal experiences are, after all, the rudimentary foundation of job shadowing, informational interviewing, and networking. And the suggestions put forth remind us all that personal involvement with the family has a lot of positive impact, certainly more than a once a year "take your child to work" event.

Quite clearly the family influences provided by vignettes like these have led to a research theme that has occupied most of Krumboltz's life, whether it has been his earlier social learning theory or his more recent theories of luck and happenstance. The point is that our families are often the source of our initial career fantasies and career information, even when these are nuanced and subtle. Moreover, our families are also frequently the source of pressure that is placed on us so that we conform to family ideals about careers, status, and the world of work.

Probably everyone can weave some tale about the impact their family had on their thoughts about an apprenticeship, part-time job, college major, internship, job, or career. Perhaps many people can put themselves in these examples. And, while people are willing to blame their families for misdirection, they also credit them for their sacrifices in helping them to achieve their career or life goals, even if those are not what they originally had in mind.

Why Hasn't There Been Much Attention Devoted to This Subject Area in Counselor Education?

These examples all point to the common theme of this book. The family appears to be a powerful variable in the decision making process, at least anecdotally as we have observed so far. So why have career counselors and researchers not given much attention to the family in the career decision making process? There are probably several answers.

Training of Counselors

First, career counselors, in their graduate degree programs, are given course work that doesn't cover material that is considered to be emotional, personal, or familial. That has probably been a mistake. Career counseling classes are replete with information about the utility of skills, interests, values, and personal characteristics in the career counseling process. But family issues are seldom acknowledged or addressed.

When career counselors are asked to take classes in family counseling or therapy, the course material infrequently, if ever, focuses upon the family influences in making career choices. Instead, the courses habitually include material on different theories of family therapy and abound with information on family dysfunction and abuse. Material on communication, triangulation, family values, power struggles, and, of course, alcohol and substance abuse are the grist for the mill in most of the pedagogy. Throw in some material on family assessment devices and a little more on intervention techniques and the result is that career counseling students receive little, if any, information on how the family affects career choice.

Furthermore, the classes that the career counseling students attend are also enrolled with students from mental health, school counseling, community counseling, family therapy, and marriage counseling majors. The career students avidly complain that they feel overwhelmed by the presence of the larger number of "personal counseling" students and object that career issues in the family system are rarely, if ever, covered. It's probably also safe to say that the family therapy classes probably don't assist much in understanding why people choose the life partners they do. But that's another matter.

Internships and Supervision

Second, in the types of internship placements that career counseling students enter, there isn't much of an opportunity for them to inquire into their clients' personal issues. There's even less chance of finding out about the influence of their clients' families on career choices. The internships or field experiences focus upon career and life planning, college advising about which courses to take, testing or assessment, academic probation, the utilization of on-line resources, and some imaginative planning about what graduates should do, eventually, with their college degrees.

Third, the supervisors of career counseling interns have not had the education or training to partake in creating a more intensified integration of personal, family, and career material, so the mechanism that is currently established is the one that prevails. And it iterates on itself. The only way that this cycle is going to be broken is if a counseling supervisor or student is willing to take the risk to try to add more personal and family focus to the counseling internship and supervisory process without acting in a manner that suggests going beyond the scope of practice.

Beliefs and Professional Orientation

Fourth, there needs to be a belief among counselors that there is some merit in intertwining personal and family issues in their study of the career decision making process. In order for that to take place there needs to be a shift in the attitudes of counselor educators and supervisors. They need to be the ones to try to redesign family therapy classes to cover case material on the family influences on career choice. At the same time, career psychologists and professors need to add more personal material to their classes in career counseling. This may already be starting to take place as newer career counseling theories—narrative career counseling, constructive career counseling, contextual career counseling, planned happenstance, and positive uncertainty, among others—are being included in career counseling courses.

Fifth, students in the field need some new techniques in order to move in a direction that incorporates the family into the process. That need highlights another purpose of this book. The material that will be included in later chapters will be an attempt to offer information on current research, but also offer to both career as well as personal counselors new ideas and devices to assist in examining the influence of the family on the career decision making process.

For now it might be productive to substantiate how your family has influenced your own career path.

What Are the Particular Experiences That Influenced Your Career and Educational Choices?

As you go through the following exercise, try to reflect in some depth about your own career choice and the influence that others may have had on it. As you consider the examples presented so far, you might also direct your attention to the caring people and landmark events in your family that affected some of your private career and educational choices.

Exercise

Here are some questions that may prick your own brain to help you to get a handle on the influence of your family of origin on your own early career and educational planning. While you complete this exercise and others that come along in the book, you might want to keep a journal for yourself as a personal guide and memory bank. By the way, these are also useful questions for career counselors and coaches to ask clients who may be interested in learning more about their family's influence.

I typically ask for this information from all of my clients.

- What activities do you remember being attracted to before the age of five?
    - Did your parents ever tell you they enjoyed the same activities when they were five?
    - Did your parents enjoy watching you in your activities?

- What do you recall wanting to be when you were in the following life stages or transitions?
    - Kindergarten
    - Sixth grade
    - 9th grade
    - High school graduation
    - College sophomore
    - College graduation

- Did you discuss any of these fantasized choices with your family?
    - If you did, what was the outcome of the discussion about the choices?

- What special talents or skills did you have that you would have liked to take advantage of?
    - Did anyone else in your family also have these special skills and talents?

- How do you recall being treated by your family with regard to your educational or career choices?
    - Did anyone recommend that you take unusually selective courses like ancient Latin or modern Mandarin?

- Did your family give you the kind of verbal support that made you feel as if you could be anything that you wanted to be?

- How much encouragement were you given to pursue whatever you wanted?

Now that you've completed the exercise, how did the questions make you feel about the influence of your family? Were you able to recognize how the formation of your own path may have been affected somewhat unconsciously by your parents? Sometimes people find that answers to questions like these above suggest that attention, or lack thereof, as well as family attitudes and values can have an adverse or highly positive effect on the career decision making process.

Why Wasn't Family Influence Focused Upon Until Recently?

Over the years careers in the United States have moved from work that was predominately rural to work that is predominately manufacturing and service. In a rural economy, most children follow in their parents' footpaths and pursue work that's either an element of a family farm or support business or a part of a more close-knit community that the family lives in. The family and the community of support are the models for most decision making.

Later, with the movements in America from a rural to a more industrialized economy, people's careers were not only in farming but also in new companies that became part of a growing landscape. The company town emerged with factories that often defined them. Communities could be described by the businesses that supported them. Harvesting natural resources like gas, iron, coal or oil, or manufacturing textiles and other goods like automobiles, tires, and steel saw individuals working with new opportunities. Company towns sprouted everywhere.

Family members with their extended relatives prospered in many of these places. Accordingly, individuals tended to follow the paths of the family members, expecting to be provided for by the company bosses. A new status emerged that was related to the work a person did, the income that was tied to it, and the business relationships that were forged. Families made sure that everyone was taken care of. There was a trust that security and income would be available to those who maintained good relationships with the owners of manufacturing services and, the family had a considerable role in perpetuating those relationships.

When company towns expanded into larger cities, residents came to serve in other occupations such as police or fire departments, health care, and education. They tended to follow in the tracks of their families, staying close to home. Even today, there are stereotypic examples of Irish fire fighters and police officers who are the fourth and fifth generations of their families.

As a service economy emerged and the manufacturing sector declined, and with new jobs expanding in different regions across the country, people began to seek opportunities at odds with those in which their family had participated. The field of career counseling was created to assist people in finding new work. People took risks in starting new businesses. Self-employment that had been a part of the rural and agricultural fabric of the country emerged again in the creation of new, small professional endeavors. An entrepreneurial, individualistic spirit had been planted in the work force, and career counseling nurtured the development of that spirit.

With the advent of air travel and the greater degree of mobility for everyone, more choices became available and younger people decided moving from their home towns gave greater opportunities and more security than what their families had before. Still, many remained behind and with career choices limited, children tended to do what their family members had done before. This way of life was predominate.

In the last half of the 20th century, increased mobility, the Civil Rights Act of 1964, increases in the number of women in the workforce, and the explosion in the numbers of two career families created a spectacle of change in how people viewed work and how they balanced opportunities with the expectations of their families. The older tracks of following the relatives into job opportunities changed dramatically to new paths where individuals sought advice on opportunities in emerging markets, quite different from what had been experienced by generations before.

At the same time, the end of World War II and the Korean and Vietnam wars brought an increase in the number of refugees and immigrants, individuals who were dependent upon the extended family members for housing, some economic support, and possible job placement. Regarding family influence, their experiences resembled that of U.S. citizens of the early 19th century.

The 21st century has seen a change in the work ethic. The downsizing and eventual demise of some manufacturing industries, the greater use of machinery and technology, globalization, and the bust of the dot coms have forced a rethinking of the notion of work and careers. The family members of the last 50 years have seen a series of business cycles that have been related to world turmoil of a military, global, and economic nature. Correspondingly, career development is now seen in the context of other world changes. Some of these changes may be social and economic while others are orchestrated by technology, globalization, and outsourcing. And individual career development has become much more unpredictable, contextual, and relational.

The field of career counseling, which began with incipient job placement services, has emerged into a profession that helps people take advantage of life's serendipitous events while adding meaning to what we all do to make a living. Career counselors, more than ever, need to add the ingredient of family influence in their study and in their work.

Why is Family Influence More Important Now Than Ever Before?

Choices

In light of the shifts in the workplace landscape, probably the first response that comes to mind in answering this question is that people today have more choices than ever. Fact is, there's an abundance of choices regarding careers today. New careers and jobs seem to be popping up at breakneck speed. Some venture capital companies offer big idea hunts to try to get inventors and investors together as they strive to take some innovative product or idea into the marketplace. But, with every potential opportunity there is the looming threat of failure.

Opportunities are open to women and minorities in spite of the fact that there are still the remnants of universal ethnic and social prejudice, bigotry, and a well documented glass ceiling. Yet, choices are everywhere. Transportation, clothing, in fact modern life has created a vast array of new products and opportunities. Look around at the variety of ipods, handheld palm pilots, and video enhanced cell phones.

With so many options, you'd expect that people would be enjoying their many freedoms to choose. But the evidence is that we all have a decreased sense of well being. Lerner (2000) has reported that the mental health issues surrounding anxiety alone cost more than $42 billion per year. And of the 23 million people who have some kind of anxiety disorder, half are phobic (Chope, 2001b). With the fears that have been wrought since 9-11 and with the daunting crush of some aspects of the technology sector, like identity theft, people are more wary and protective of themselves and their careers.

The many new choices we all share have come with rapid changes in the workplace and the manner in which business is conducted today. I recommended earlier (Chope, 2000) that people need to begin to accept instability in the work world. By doing this they will begin to have more realistic expectations regarding their opportunities. There are words in the career and employment counselors' vocabulary that are certainly recent additions. Globalization, outsourcing, "jobless recovery," job sharing, team building, and the end of work as we know it (Rifkin, 1995) have been well talked about and chronicled. While the outsourcing and globalization of business create new challenges, they will also create new opportunities.

As we become freer to choose what we want, we seem to be less happy, so we fall back on lessons from the family. What risks should we take and what can we learn from our family histories? Family members who have been through past business cycles and the current business changes believe they are in a stronger position to offer advice. Moreover, a look at several generations of family members allows clients and counselors to gather different perspectives on the family characteristics. There can be evidence of families that are enterprising, or socially committed, entrepreneurial or creative. A few generations ago, these patterns wouldn't have been so meaningful, even if they had been available.

Career Theory Focus Has Been on the Individual, But That May Be Changing

To be sure, in our culture, it's the individual child or family member who eventually makes the choices. And for much of the history of the United States, a focus upon individualism regarding choices was a basic tenet (Gysbers, Heppner, & Johnston, 2003). Separation from the family is thought of as an important development task and has been discussed at length by family therapists (Bowlby, 1982). But Gysbers et al. point to the demands of individualism as they note that career theories are "theories of the self." And when you think of it, can there be anything that is really more personal and private than deciding what you are going to do or be for the rest of your life?

Unfortunately, career counseling focused upon the individual because career theories also focused upon the individual. More recently, however, the Zeitgeist has turned and new career theories have been recently developed that are departures from earlier approaches. Lately, some researchers have suggested categorizing into two groups, positivist theories and post modern theories (Vondracek & Kawasaki, 1995).

Positivism and Post Modernism

The positivist theories explore the relationship of the individual to the world of work. These theories focus upon models of goodness of fit or empowerment to ensure that the working individual can be involved in activities that build self-esteem while leading to self-actualization. For example, developmental theories focus upon the utilization of data to understand how an individual moves through particular stages, confronting developmental tasks along the way that help to shape and transform the individual into someone who has continuity with the past while navigating the present, and considering the future.

Psychological and career testing, the hallmarks of many career theories, are used in a positivistic way to validate theories as much as they are used for exploratory purposes by the individual. But no tests except for perhaps the environment scales of Rudy Moos (1986, Moos &

Moos, 1981) really focus upon the family to assist in career decision making. Gysbers et al. (2003) add to this by pointing out that in the computerized career information system DISCOVER, there are many questions that cover material on individual interests and abilities and other personal characteristics. But there are no questions that directly assess culture or family in career decision making. With all of the money devoted to the new and expanded O*NET, the same problem holds true. Searching questions about the family are never asked.

On the other hand, an opportunity is emerging for counselors to go somewhat beyond what has been offered in the positivistic theories. Alternative, post modern theories force individuals to give a greater degree of meaning to the career decision making experience. The phrase "meaning making" is used to give definition to the quest for the individual as he or she pursues a dream through the world of work and relationships. The use of the term "post modern" has been suggested by Niles and Harris-Bowlsbey (2002) to categorize newer career development approaches. These include three approaches: narrative counseling, constructivist career counseling, and contextualized career counseling.

Briefly, among a variety of information sources, narrative counseling utilizes family material in the development of continuity over a lifetime (Cochran, 1997). In the contextual explanation of career choice (Young, Valach, & Collin, 1996), counselors incorporate material that includes family, culture, heritage, environmental issues, and economics. There's a focus upon the meaning making that occurs with the interaction between the individual and the environment. To bring this down to practicality, Niles and Harris-Bowlsbey illustrate that even in a straightforward discussion between high school students and their parents, a wealth of clinically useful information can be garnered. Not only can information about the career world be discussed but also the feelings that each party has toward the other's ideas. And both the parents and the students can be given an opportunity to create their own meaning about the experience.

Recall that Jack London and Zac Unger tried to create meaningful lives as rugged individuals to give meaning. And their mothers supported them while concurrently assisting them in forging new career paths. Their parents also wanted to help them to derive meaning. They both added meaning to their lives by becoming writers; their individualism was communicated in fantasies and fiction about others.

The Family Structure Has Been Altered

The family itself has been undergoing an interesting alteration as well and deserves new attention in the context of career development.

Zedack and Mosier (1990) have pointed out that the "traditional nuclear family accounts for less than 20% of households in the United States." And further they report that "the traditional picture of a male wage earner committed to the support of a wife and several children makes up only about 11% of all families" (Zedack & Mosier, 1990, p. 240). They go on to say that the most profound change in the work force is in the dual career family and note that "about 40% of the work force is comprised of dual earner couples and another 6% are single parents."

Two other factors are important in understanding the role of the family. First, the family is undergoing some challenging rethinking and redefinition. There are increasing numbers of gay and lesbian partnerships and attempts to legalize same sex marriages. Domestic partner laws exist in some states like Vermont and in many large cities like San Francisco. These relationships bring a whole new dimension to understanding the impact of family on career decision making. Some people think that the concept of traditional marriage and the family is in terrible straits, exemplified by President George W. Bush's proposition to create a constitutional amendment to preserve the sanctity of marriage and family. So the complexity of family combinations and partnerships, step parents, adoptive parents, dual career or dual income families, or single parent families has become more intricate. The "Brady Bunch" has become an acceptable norm, exemplified by the blended family of presidential candidate and Massachusetts Senator John Kerry.

Further, with individuals living longer, with improved health technology and care, there is a new generation of people evolving popularly referred to as the "sandwich generation." Middle-aged family members have been thrown the task of caring for aging parents and supporting them. Feeling the financial squeeze, these folks must also expend resources on their children, especially regarding their health care and postsecondary education. And, both health care and education are expensive and, with many state budget crises, in some degree of turmoil. This results in added stress and distinct feelings among younger family members that they should go out and help to earn income to support the family. So everyone is feeling the press of the "sandwich generation." College students are taking longer to complete their education as many work part-time to support themselves to take away financial burdens from their families.

What Role Has Our Awareness of Multiculturalism Played?

Changing population demographics, the influx of immigrants after World War II, the Korean War, and the Vietnam War, globalization, and cultural pluralism are among some of the influences that have led to the development of multicultural awareness and counseling. By some estimates (Niles & Harris-Bowlsbey, 2002) nonwhites, women, and immigrants were more than five-sixths of the net addition to the workforce in the last 15 years of the 20th century. There are newsworthy investigations regularly about the unemployment of particular ethnic groups, especially African Americans and Native Americans, and the prevalent discrimination against gays, lesbians, and people with disabilities.

The career development processes that are discussed in most career theories are written with a particular context in mind according to Gysbers, Heppner, and Johnston (2003). They point to five key tenets of career development theories and interventions: individualism and autonomy, affluence, structure of opportunity open to all, the centrality of work in people's lives, and the linearity, progressiveness, and rationality of the career development process. People from different cultures may not share the world view that incorporates all or some of these tenets. Clearly that doesn't mean that we need to throw all career theories out with the bath water. But it does suggest that the use of all theories of career choice and the selection of interventions need to be done with knowledge and integration of multicultural perspectives.

What this emphasizes for our purposes is that the world views of different cultures will be reflected in how different roles are played out in the family. Whether there is individualism or collectivism, there will be expectations regarding the children and the elders in the family. Some cultures will want children to be independent, while others will want them to stay at home for as long as possible. Some children will be expected to improve the lifestyle of their parents, while others will not have any responsibilities. Quite a few children will assume roles in family businesses. Differences in culture and lifestyle and sexual orientation will be important to consider whether the client's level of acculturation is similar to the family of origin or not.

Conclusion

The past 15 years or so have been witness to substantial increases in understanding the role that relationships play in career choice, job satisfaction, and general work adjustment. While this is certainly due to a variety of factors, without question the greater degree of interest in feminist perspectives, multiculturalism, and attachment theory has probably had a major impact.

Career planning, life planning, and advancement appear to be a multifaceted developmental, learning, and cognitive process. When clients arrive for consultation, they bring a load of historical baggage with them.

Some of this has been learned from significant family relationships while some has been the result of contextual variables like family environment, social and economic status, and education. How clients gather information, assess themselves, learn about the alternatives in the educational and labor markets, maneuver themselves through different educational and career choices, and create long- and short-term plans are all dependent upon how well they have utilized the available knowledge and information from their personal histories.

Probably one place where the family has an enormous influence is in the restriction of career options. This is well depicted in the 1999 film *October Sky* directed by Joe Johnston. It's the true story of Homer Hickam, a West Virginia teen who wanted to become a rocket scientist against the wishes of his father. Young men in the small towns of West Virginia were expected to spend their career in the coal mines. Confronting that reality, as Homer did, in order to pursue his passion for launching rockets created a whole new set of family and community conflicts.

Blustein (1992) points out that whereas career development is a lifelong process, it doesn't have any firm crystallization until late adolescence or young adulthood. And, for some, late adolescence can be protracted. Against this backdrop, there is the unfortunate pressure that is placed upon individuals, like Homer Hickam, to begin to make career decisions when they may not be ready. In some freshman high school classes, students are asked to prepare career books and papers, reflecting what they may want to do after high school and college. Parents, knowing the cost of higher education, want to ensure that their children are getting the most for their dollars and as such want to have their children solidify their plans. Most tell me that they want their sons and daughters to finish college in four years. But this certainly takes away from people engaging in exploring alternative activities and majors while putting a limit on appropriately extensive planning. Probably the greatest gift that the family can give is the opportunity to explore alternatives. With this present, people can focus upon their transferable skills.

So what should be explored when considering how the family is influential? First, the developmental process is important, especially as it relates to the impact of the family in the formative years. How competencies, skills, and self-esteem germinate in the context of the family is essential to understand. Knowing how these attributes were developed is essential. Accordingly, counselors should inquire about their clients' experience with chores in the home, term time and summer employment, organized athletics, Boys and Girls Clubs, Scouts, religious affiliations, and the like. Then, they should ask about family involvement in these activities to determine how the clients were taught to explore, network, and partake of opportunities with family support.

Second, the family is the county seat of learning. Mitchell and Krumboltz (1990) point to the nature of learning and how it affects interests, skills, and self concept. People become interested in activities as they are exposed to them, and the degree to which the family focuses upon broadening learning activities affects how individuals can conceptualize and fantasize about future opportunities.

The contextual variables from the family probably affect the career decision making process the most. The social and economic status of the family, geography, the community, quality of the educational system, stability and comfort in the home, role models, technology, how many workers were in the family, accommodations for members of the family including children and elders, illness, absent parent or a traveling parent, and desire to have it all are variables worth discussing.

Chapter Summary

Through brief biographies and clinical examples, this chapter has demonstrated why the influence of the family in career decision making is so important. Suggestions have been offered for how influential family material might be incorporated into counseling training programs and clinical career counseling practice. Opportunities were created for readers to explore their own family and the influence it had in the career decision making process.

Chapter 2

An Update on Current Research

"If we knew what we were doing, it wouldn't be called research, would it?"
Albert Einstein

There have been two important reviews, in 1984 and 2004, of the literature on family influence in career decision making. These two reviews are summarized in this chapter. In addition, a special issue on family influence from a journal devoted to counseling applications is also discussed. Directions for future research, including the interface between work and relationships, are suggested.

The Importance of Research

There are two major contributions that researchers make toward understanding any topic. One is conceptual and the other is empirical. Conceptually, researchers have taught us approaches and perspectives, while giving us paradigms with which to view problems and subjects. Researchers categorize and organize the ways we view and understand behavior, for example, parents' child rearing activities. Both practitioners and researchers often develop concepts and constructs that allow for the formulation of theories. Then they try to confirm the validity of these theories with data.

Data remain the staunch empirical contribution to research. They're the facts and figures researchers obtain to help to confirm and promote theoretical notions and hypothetical constructs, the wild ideas of science. The relevance, appropriateness, and generalizability of data allow practitioners and researchers to make judgments about the strength and applicability of different theories and their accompanying constructs. Data allow us to go beyond the mere telling of folk tales and creation of beliefs about the behavior we are interested in. They're used to support or confirm our ideas, paradigms, and beliefs. Gathering data about the influence of the family in career decision making may help to add to a systematic understanding of how and why people make some of the decisions that they do. Career counselors can develop new clinical techniques based on these understandings.

The available research focusing on family influence in career decision making is ironically voluminous but topically scattered, readily available but with an uneven usefulness. Nevertheless, it lays a foundation for practitioners and researchers who want to gather information to broaden their understanding of this important aspect of career decision making.

Does Family Influence Really Matter?

Some of the material in Chapter 1 suggests that no matter how you cut it, parents frequently appear to have a profound influence on the intellectual, social, and emotional components of their children's lives. Laurence Steinberg (2004) has made it abundantly clear that kids don't raise themselves. So, in most cases the guidance that parents offer, inadvertent as well as conscious, becomes a powerful component in the nature of the decision making process that their offspring develop, along with the variety of career choices that are made available to them.

That parents influence their children in this way is, however, sometimes controversial, because there are examples where it may not be entirely accurate. Judith Rich Harris (1998) is well known for her seminal work in questioning assumptions about nurturing and the effect that parents have on their children. Needless to say, her work continues to raise eyebrows while generating research that both confirms and disputes her premises. She is undoubtedly correct when she suggests, along with the behavior geneticists, that DNA accounts for about 50% of the behavioral patterns we witness in people. This isn't exactly a novel idea considering for many years the heritability of personality has fallen around 50%.

But Harris has an interesting perspective on family influence. She posits that parents can clearly have an effect on their children. But she also suggests that children have an effect on their parents, so that parenting style is an interactive behavior pattern brought about by both the parenting style as well as the behavior of the children. She points out that in the attempt to measure the effect of parenting on children, researchers may also be measuring the effects of children on parenting skills. The problem is, we can't be too sure which is the more powerful.

Parents don't necessarily engage in the same parenting behaviors with all of their children, but in fact adjust their behavior depending on the degree of difficulty of the child and the legacy that they have established with other children. For example, firstborn children are nurtured differently than second and third children. Accordingly, the analysis of the research data that are being used to measure and describe general family influence may not always be presenting a completely accurate measure of what is really happening to all of the children in the same home. That's why individual narratives may be necessary for extracting information about the family dynamics that are related to that child's career decision making.

Harris does believe in the impact of context on the behavior of children. Much of the work in career decision making is focusing upon contextual issues. But, unlike many career development researchers, she suggests that "significant others" in addition to the parents need to be studied in understanding child development. For example, the peers of children, teachers, coaches, choir leaders, and Scout leaders may be as influential as parents.

This contextual material has not been well studied because it's usually too difficult to obtain except in small samples where different respondents are interviewed in depth. Too, children, especially adolescents, tend to keep their home lives and peer group lives separate and unidentified. So researchers don't often focus upon contextual variables like peer groups and significant others outside the family.

What will be shown in some of the career development literature that follows is that socioeconomic status is related to career choice. But what the researchers fail to examine is whether it is the socioeconomic status of the peer group, or the school setting, or the neighborhood, or the parent group that has the most impact. Most likely they are all influential. However, Harris points out the complexity involved in looking at family influence; her book and papers may eventually change the way research is done on context and family influence. Nevertheless, she concludes that as we consider family influences, we should be thinking about three additional variables that go beyond simple family influence: genetic determination, the effects of children on parenting, and the effect of peer groups as moderators of career choices and aspirations.

These three variables are all among the components of the relational context in career decision making that has recently been considered for study. A major contribution to this effort is Blustein's work on the interface between work and relationships (2001). Here the work captures the influence of not just family, but also peers and other cohorts who impact the career decision making process. Blustein also suggests that we explore who is asked for advice in this process and who is kept out of it.

Where Do Families Have an Influence?

In the vast number of cases presented in this book, families appear to have a great deal of influence. In my clinical work and reading of biographies, I am struck by the power of this influence. But I also believe that we are at the front end of serious study in this area. Additional analyses of biographies and reporting of case materials would help support some ideas offered. Continued study could also help to refocus the field. Ongoing research can help to contribute to a systematic approach to theory building and data collecting while alerting us to important contextual factors that may have been overlooked in cases, where families appear to influence their children behaviorally,

Throughout his career, Donald Super (1957, 1963, 1984) believed that the contextual variables provided by the family had an overarching determinant of an individual's career development. And other researchers have suggested that the family, indeed, be given much more focus in understanding career decision making and life planning (Blustein, Walbridge, Friedlander, & Palladino, 1991; Herr and Lear, 1984).

Super's well known contemporary, Ann Roe (1957), studied the role of the family, with rather mixed results, as she related child rearing determinants to career choices. She understood that people seemed to be inculcated with two basic orientations: they either moved away from people or toward them in the development of their vocational interests and occupational choices. These two orientations, she believed, were affected by parental attitudes and parent child interaction. Unfortunately, at the time of her theorizing, she didn't have the data to support her contentions.

Interestingly, career theories, especially those of a developmental nature like Super's (1957), suggest that family attitudes toward work along with the interpersonal relationships in the family affect how people choose careers and how they adjust to them afterwards. Others imply that there is some type of ongoing interactive relationship between family variables and the career decisions that offspring make, reinforcing the argument that the family plays an increasingly salient but complex role in career decision making (Kinnier, Brigman, & Noble, 1990).

With the interactive possibilities in mind, a few researchers (Blustein et al., 1991) have spent time exploring different models like Bowen's (1978) family systems theory and Bowlby's (1982) attachment theory to try to conceptualize developmental evidence for a relationship between family and career decision making outcomes. These efforts have resulted in some interesting studies linking interest development to childhood attachment. For example, research linking attachment styles to Holland's typology (Johnson, Thompson, McCrudden, & Franklin, 1998) has suggested that insecurely attached people appear to be more realistic, conventional, or investigative while more securely attached people represent the entire range of code types.

Where Can Research Information About Family Influence Be Found?

I've chosen to answer this question with four important sources of literature on the influence of the family on career development. While there are other papers, monographs and books, none has focused as distinctively on family influence as these do. The first two of these sources are literature reviews that cover the most important published papers and research findings available, although they exclude empirical studies that have been presented in paper and poster sessions at state and national conventions like the National Career Development Association, American Counseling Association, and American Psychological Association. The third important literature source is a special issue of the *Career Planning and Adult Development Journal* (Gelardin, 2001) containing original articles exploring the influence of family on career choice. The fourth is the issue of *The Counseling Psychologist* (Blustein, 2001) that is devoted almost entirely to the study of relationships and work.

The first literature review was prepared by Schulenberg, Vondracek, and Crouter in 1984 and was, until recently, the only substantial review available on research covering family influence on career decision making. This older research on the influence of the family on career decision making examined the impact of structural variables like socioeconomic status, birth order, and gender. The review also explored process variables that may affect career choice like modeling, parental support, and parenting styles. The review represented a useful collection.

A new review by Whiston and Keller was published in 2004. It summarized the findings from 77 studies related to the influence of the family of origin on career development. This work represents 29 different journals from a number of varying disciplines including psychology, education, counseling and guidance, and career development. A large body of this work will be summarized herein.

The third piece of relevant literature for those interested in the application of research is the *Career Planning and Adult Development Journal* special issue editorial work of Gelardin (2001). Unlike the other reviews, this entire issue was devoted to family issues, but it went beyond more narrow studies of career influence. The collection is quite a bit different from the 1984 and 2004 reviews. It was prepared as a response to the 9-11 terrorists attacks and devoted to the need to understand family and "real world" connections in making important decisions. For example, the work included discussions of the "sandwich generation" and older workers. In addition, there were articles on the complex career development issues in family owned businesses.

Finally the March 2001 issue of *The Counseling Psychologist* (Blustein, 2001) addresses some of the most complex issues associated with the relational influences in career decision making. Some of the material is extracted from interviews on relational contexts, and other material is drawn from a reanalysis of case material presented over several years in the *Career Development Quarterly*.

What Have We Learned From the Literature Reviews?

One of the striking aspects of reviewing the literature on family influence is that many of the studies have often provided vague, conflicting, and nondefinitive results. This remains the case even with current work. To illustrate, some studies expound that there is support linking family of origin issues to the career decision making process (Kinnier, Birgman, & Noble, 1990) while others profess to find none or only a minimal connection (Eigen, Hartman, & Hartman, 1987). Still, in spite of these less than conclusive results, for 50 years most career theorists have given a nod to the notion that the family does indeed influence the career planning and decision making process.

The 1984 and 2004 literature reviews provide an excellent summary and analysis of the findings of the 50 years or so of research in this area. We will begin with the results from Schulenberg et al. (1984) as commented upon by Whiston and Keller (2004).

Schulenberg, Vondracek, and Crouter's 1984 Research Review

The Schulenberg et al. (1984) research review handled three areas of influence: social context, family context, and family process. Those categories are used here in summarizing the review. The first area included the whereabouts of the family in a comparative social context. That area covered the influence of the family's socioeconomic status, its ethnicity, and the occupational status of the workers in the family. The second area included contextual aspects of the family like family structure and configuration, and certain other variables such as single parenthood. The third area addressed family process factors like parent-child relationships. Most of that research examined whether or not particular sons followed the occupational pursuits of their fathers.

The work described in Schulenberg et al. (1984) is, of course, dated and doesn't reflect either the cultural changes that have taken place in the United States or the changes that have taken place in career development theory. Moreover, career theory since 1984 has become more contextual and constructivist rather than positivist, as indicated throughout this book.

There are clear gaps in the research. Very little work is representative of our evolving multiethnic and multicultural society. Research on family interaction patterns has been essentially left out. These two areas, among others, will be picked up in the later review by Whiston and Keller (2004). But let's begin with the Schulenberg et al. review.

Social Context Variables. The variables of socioeconomic status of the family and the ethnicity of the individual job seeker have an effect on the occupational choices that people pursue as well as their eventual general occupational status. Occupational aspirations, as well as expectations, are also related to socioeconomic status.

Looking only at relationships and not cause and effect, it was concluded by Schulenberg et al. that those people from a lower socioeconomic status and from families that were not Caucasian ended up working in jobs that were low paying with the concomitant lower occupational status. Indeed, some of the research reads like a discussion of the obvious. Still, at least one study suggested that family background characteristics like these may not be as influential or important as people may think. Intriguingly, research that has come after 1984 has shown a noticeable decline in studies related to the interaction between socioeconomic status and career decision making.

Ethnicity seems to be a major factor impacting career choice, job aspirations, and vocational outcome. However, much of the research that was reported on in 1984 did not have samples as diversified as those in today's journals. So generalizability and applicability regarding ethnicity was a problem.

Gender, especially in studies of social modeling, played an interesting role in the early research and apparently does today as well. Several studies examined the results of social modeling. Mothers who worked outside the home tended to raise daughters who worked outside the home. Girls were influenced in their aspirations by the occupations of both parents while boys were influenced more by the occupations of their fathers. Gender interacted with social class. In contrast to the experience of girls from more elevated socioeconomic levels, girls from lower socioeconomic backgrounds selected occupations that asked for less education.

Family Context Variables. Apparently only a few structural variables seemed to influence career choice; these were related to family size and birth order. Larger families tended to produce children who had less ambitious educational and occupational expectations. They also did not go as far with their education as children from smaller families and ended up in occupations that were lower paying.

Although, birth order has been seen in the theoretical literature as an influential variable for consideration, particularly among Adlerians, the studies reviewed didn't support that notion.

Family Process Factors. The 1970s were witness to research efforts that tried to associate family process variables with the career development of women. This was rich territory at the time because of employment changes brought about by the Civil Rights Act of 1964 and the Women's Movement which captured the attention of the workforce in the 1960s and 1970s. It also interacted with social modeling research. Women who decided at the time to pursue work that would be considered "non traditional" saw themselves as more similar to their fathers than to their mothers. But women who pursued paths very different from either parent were able to do so more easily, if they felt support from their mothers. In addition, women who pursued nontraditional paths came from families who valued ambitious educational and vocational pursuits. They were also from a higher socioeconomic plane.

Students in college appeared to follow career paths of their parents. However, when they diverged from their parents' occupations, particularly boys, they selected occupations that had characteristics similar to their fathers. For example, work tasks, earnings, and autonomy on the job were similar in the occupational characteristics of jobs chosen by boys even though the job titles were dissimilar from their father's. Identification with either or both parents influenced the direction of the children's careers.

Except for the work of Ann Roe which was referred to previously, the study of family interaction patterns has been given very little attention. That has been changing more recently and makes the Whiston and Keller review noteworthy. A more recent paper (Hartung, Lewis, May, & Niles, 2000) summarizes a body of evidence suggesting that the way family members interact and their patterns of interaction does show a relationship to the career decision making process.

Other research summarized by Schulenberg et al. points to middle and upper class children as preferring to work in experiences that value self-direction, while more lower class children appear to value conformity. This has been characterized as evidence that lower class children are punished more frequently to get them to conform to certain societal standards.

Whiston and Keller's 2004 Research Review

The sociocultural changes that have taken place in the past 25 years demanded an updated review of research. Better samples, higher level statistical techniques, and greater awareness of the multicultural and multiethnic employment aspects of the country have led to new research. In addition, there was a need for more work of a process driven nature. This has been reviewed by Whiston and Keller (2004). Using the organizational categories from their major contribution, some of the findings about family influence are enumerated below.

Children's Career Development. The research articles summarized articulated unmistakable genetic influences in the development of career related interests. This is hardly surprising given the influence of the research summarized earlier by Harris (1998). Examples presented in this book, including many stories of musicians, sports heroes, and health care workers, show a clear predisposition for children to have the genetically given talents of their parents. Of course, some of these skills may have been enhanced by the parents' interest in nurturing specific abilities in their children. What child doesn't remember being pressured to partake of unwanted skill development?

Direct suggestions made to elementary school children related to occupational direction apparently have some influence on their career decisions. And children from two parent homes were more likely to express occupational preferences in contrast to children who were in single parent situations, living with other relatives, or residing in foster care situations.

The data are mixed concerning the influence of the gender of parents relative to career choice. In some cases, mothers' careers seem to be more influential than fathers' in the career aspirations of the children. Yet, this influence diminishes by the sixth grade. Children will, however, aspire to a mother's occupational status if that status appears to be higher than the status of the father. But, when the occupational status of the mother and father are equal, girls were not influenced by either gender while boys seemed to be influenced by their mother. It should also be noted that as children age through the elementary school years, they appear to take more ownership over their career aspirations, reporting more of their own aspirations rather than the aspirations that their parents had for them.

Still, many elementary students desire to pursue the occupations of their parents even though they say that this is their own choice. Girls who perceived their mothers as having some degree of power in the family also viewed more careers as being available to both men and women and preferred aspirations that were less traditionally identified with women. In these studies, regardless of gender or ethnicity, members of the extended family didn't play a significant role on career aspirations.

So, parents appear to influence the children in the early preadolescent years, though this influence dwindles some as the children approach middle adolescence. Employed mothers seem to impact the perceived career options of both girls and boys. And those from non two-parent homes seem to feel less maneuverability regarding their career aspirations than those from two parent homes.

Adolescent Career Development. There are almost three times as many studies available exploring the family influence on adolescents as there are on children. The later research in the area suggests that studying the influence of structural variables like socioeconomic status and ethnicity is quite complex with modern families and difficult to proclaim definitive results from. Clearly there continues to be a need for studies that explore structural family variables, particularly in the realm of multiculturalism.

Not surprisingly, high level educational and occupational aspirations are associated with family environments that are supportive and where the parents have a high degree of expectation for their adolescent children. This is true for both boys and girls. As with studies with children, parental occupations are tied to the interests of their adolescent children. Adolescents from professional and skilled families tend to have broader interests than those families who work in unskilled trades, suggesting that adolescents from unskilled families may make career decisions prematurely.

One study described by Whiston and Keller stands out from the others both in technique and conclusions. Young and Friesen (1992), using a critical incident review procedure, identified 10 categories of parental intentions among middle class parents that were used to assist with their adolescent' career development. Nine of these were focused on helping their adolescent while one, achievement of parents' personal goals, was not. The nine remaining intentions were: (1) skill acquisition, (2) acquisition of specific values or beliefs, (3) protection from unwanted experiences, (4) increasing independent thinking or action, (5) decreasing sex-role stereotyping, (6) moderation of parent-child relationships, (7) facilitation of human relationships, (8) enhancement of character development, and (9) development of personal responsibility.

Expanding upon this research, Young and other colleagues (Young, Valach, & Collin, 1996) found that career dialogues between parents and adolescents were more effective when there were shared goals, open communication, clear methods to accomplish goals, parents served as leaders and the adolescents were individuated from their parents. But again, these results have complex interactions with social context variables and were extracted from predominantly middle class families. It is unclear what factors would be as important among families that suffered the ravages of discrimination and very low pay. In addition, where there are now so many single family households, it is unclear as to how some of these factors would hold up in their circumstances.

Suffice it to say, more research is needed in this realm, especially work that embraces multicultural samples and narrative approaches to data gathering rather than using highly structured measuring instruments. In any event, it seems clear that parental attitudes and expectations appear to be related to adolescent career aspirations and that these variables may be more significant than the structural variables of family class, size, and salaries. Family support, the perception of opportunities, and education and occupations of the parents all influenced the aspirations of adolescent children. In fact, parental expectations continue to be the single most powerful variable related to family influence. These expectations and aspirations also check out cross culturally, although non-Caucasian families did not show the same degree of significance with regard to the influence of expectations and aspirations.

While the research points to some degree to directions of family influence, many of the results of the studies have a tendency to be a discussion of the obvious. If any breakthrough can be taken from these data, it is that counselors should assist parents to become more interactive and responsive to their children. Counselors could play a role in coaching parents to develop appropriate listening skills, involving themselves with their adolescents' lives without smothering them or creating an enmeshed family system, making individuation impossible.

College Students. Whiston and Keller reported on 32 studies that demonstrated family influence on college students and young adults who may have already entered the workforce or pursued a vocational-technical education. Unfortunately, there are very few studies of non college bound students or young adults, a generic truth in the career counseling literature. And there is a dearth of information on multicultural college students. Yet in those cases that extracted information from multicultural families, parental support was perceived to be a major factor in their career development.

Nonetheless, with what is available, as in the other categories, many of the conclusions that are reached in these studies would not be surprising to most people. Young adults who have the highest levels of career commitment appear to be those who are secure in their attachment to their parents and have few family conflicts.

A further study by Young and his colleagues (Young, Friesen, & Borycki, 1994) provided some of the most salient material on family influence. Examining family influence using family narratives, they categorized five ways that parents influenced the career development of their children, whether that was in a positive or negative way. These were:

1. Progressive narrative with a dramatic turning point
2. Progressive narrative with a positive evaluation frame
3. Progressive narrative with negatively evaluated stages
4. Anticipated regressive narrative
5. The sad narrative

In the first category, Young et al. report that poor parenting had an adversive influence on their adolescents' career expectations, but a dramatic turning point had assisted the adolescents in developing clearer goals while becoming more self-reliant. This material fits in nicely with material on planned happenstance.

In the second instance, results suggest that good communication with parents about career choices was related to appropriate parental expectations. In the third instance, respondents didn't feel that their families had helped them to generate a positive outcome, while the fourth category suggested that the participants may have had initial successes but eventually were, in a sense, failures who were not going to live up to parental expectations. In the fifth category, there was little in the way of parental assistance and because of this, there was a lowering of self-esteem and hope. In this category, there was a progressive decline in the goals of the respondents.

The college student section presented evidence, for the first time, of the influence of siblings in support of career choices. Siblings were found to have both a positive and negative influence suggesting complexity in sibling support. In several cases, siblings were seen as a positive influence by providing multidimensional support. This additional support could be tangible as well as emotional, contributing to an increase in the comfort level available to the college students.

The general results of the studies show that family influence is broadened for college students, although as many as 37% of the students felt that their families did not contribute to their career decision making process. It is also true that there need to be more studies that focus upon the influence of gender in decision making. And finally, family factors like intimidation, enmeshment, and interaction need to be given more than lip service in the research literature. More and more, family stability seems to be related to career decidedness. Studies of career indecision show how indecisiveness may indeed be related to variables that characterize family dysfunction.

What has occurred so far seems to reflect that there are not guiding theories that tie the work on family influence together. The work summarized represents a large number of studies that produce data, but don't seem to use theories like family systems theory or attachment theory to frame the research. Charlene Alderfer (2004) has been critical of work related to family influence because it has not tried to work within the containers of family therapy theory. While there has been some interesting work related to the attachment theory of Bowlby, much more needs to be considered. There appear to be some relationships between the development of interests, for example, and the attachment state of mind of a respondent.

Adults. Whiston and Keller reported upon only five studies that explored the effect of family influences upon adults. Interestingly, several of these studies were done with people of color. Further, the data were not obtained with questionnaires or tests. They used, instead, retrospective interviews. The conclusions are noteworthy because they show the importance of engaging in this work from a multicultural perspective. Many of the conclusions for people of color are consistent with those of whites; however, there is an emphasis on education that appears to be stronger in families of color.

The data indicate that even as adults, there is a reliance on family members for support and communication. There is also a need for women in particular to be exposed to both traditional and nontraditional role models. Extended families can often provide this. In addition, families can be supportive, but they also provide conflicts when people are forced to choose between the wishes of their families and their own wishes. Families can play a very powerful role in the lives of people seeking careers; and there is the ingrained notion that the family is to be respected. It is also true that adults, unlike children, are influenced by both their immediate family of origin, but also by their extended family members.

There is, of course, a scarcity of material in this area prompting a call for efforts to include the studies of adults. They are probably the most difficult to study because they are not as readily available as students. However, Whiston and Keller suggest that they be made a part of more longitudinal studies.

Michael Brown (2004), supports the need for more clearly directed research in this area. He considers it an area that is ripe for research and practical investment. And he has noted that there are a variety of questions that need to be addressed. Some of these are below, and I have added a few to the list.

Some problems for researchers:
- How do we define what constitutes a family and control for this factor?
- How do we compare single parent families with nonsingle parent families? And how do we categorize gay, lesbian, bisexual, and transgender families?
- How are step and foster families different from other families of origin?
- Is family influence due more to the social and economic status of the family than to the child rearing and interaction patterns that take place?
- Is it even possible to categorize and standardize the childrearing patterns and reinforcement contingencies that parents use?
- How do we understand the nature of beliefs that families have about careers and education?
- How do we standardize and make comparable different family histories?
- What career beliefs do different family members have that expand or reduce the career options of their offspring?

As this list suggests, the biggest problem that Brown points to is the fact that there are not variables that are "defined consistently and operationalized appropriately" to lend themselves to good and consistent research (p. 589).

A Special Issue of the Career Planning and Adult Development Journal: Family Influences on Career Choice and Success

Unlike the previous material posed by literature reviews from 1984 and 2004, the material in the *Career Planning and Adult Development Journal* (Gelardin, 2001) is designed more for practitioners.

The journal's material contains strategies for counselors to assist in a variety of different circumstances, as this brief description will show. There are materials that include acknowledging the power of the family in creating a work life program in international businesses. It shows how organizations are willing to address the home life needs of employees and how programs can be developed to assist them.

There are models for developing programs for older workers who may want to do things differently than their children want. This is an interesting twist because it looks at the influence of children on their parents' career decisions, addressing the "sandwich" generation and the effect of aging families on career givers and their families. There is also material on the influence of money and different definitions of success along with new ways of gathering information about family influence. These resources also include some of my early work on the creation of a protocol to assess family influence. There are also articles on structural issues like the influence of socioeconomic status, process variables like mother/daughter relationships, and new material on unconscious motivators related to our career decisions. Finally, there is material on family business. The research literature on family influence did not provide material on family business, so this coverage provides important new information. Many multicultural families and immigrants establish family owned and operated businesses.

Future Directions

The template for the manner in which future research might be conducted on the influence of the family in career decision making was presented in a major contribution in *The Counseling Psychologist* in March 2001 (Blustein, 2001). The focus of this work was on the nature of the interface between work and relationships. What was suggested is that while the role of the family is important, there needs to be a more multidimensional approach to the work that includes the extended family and other significant others like peer groups. This is not unlike what Harris proposed.

While Blustein acknowledges the central role of work in the human experience, he joins with others who wish to add more energy to a focus on context in career counseling. The Zeitgeist is apparent from his review of the literature that from many angles—feminism, social psychology, developmental psychology, and family systems theory—there is a need for a greater understanding of the role of our relationships on our aspirations, expectations, and eventual choices of careers. He believes that to study work and relationships separately is to make simplistic the terrific complexity and synergy that is available when the two are studied together.

Blustein lays out a road map for future research and the creation of a new knowledge base. He calls for research into three domains:

1. What are the ways in which work and relationships intersect?
2. What theoretical frames can be used to conceptualize the intersection?
3. What methods should be used to engage in further exploration of these questions?

He goes ahead and introduces three articles that seek to serve as ways that future research can answer the challenges that he has put forth. Interestingly, the articles dwell on the narratives of individuals giving a greater degree of credence to this method of research and obtaining of information. This sets the stage for his demand that both researchers and practitioners appreciate the elimination of falsely developed boundaries between different experiences and instead "maintain an unbiased affirming focus on multiple contextual domains simultaneously" (p. 186). He adds that the "natural ebb and flow of life does not generally replicate the sorts of artificial categories that academic scholars have created in their work" (p. 187). For example, multicultural distinctions are established for the convenience of researchers and surveyors, but rarely reflect the cultural pluralism that many people embody.

The themes that are conveyed in this volume of the journal speak to the need to follow at least three new roads. These are studying and understanding the complexities of social support and relationships in the human experience; understanding the socioeconomic, multiethnic, and multicultural components of this experience; and developing research techniques that get to the heart of these issues. This approach is most demanding as it calls for the collection of narratives for study rather than research techniques that are more categorical and reductionistic. Training may be more contingent upon the understanding of these narratives.

Much of the contribution of this book comes from the stories of people drawn from the public press and from case illustrations that exemplify the issues that Blustein describes. How we extract information in new ways from clients will be discussed in the chapter on assessment. This book also appreciates the complexity of the work/relationship interface. The next chapter presents this in the discussion of multicultural family influences in career decision making.

Chapter Summary

This chapter has presented an overview of the most important recent research on the impact of family relationships on the career decision making process. There is clearly evidence that family support can enhance the career decision making process, while a lack of support can have an adverse impact. There is also cutting edge research carried out by Young and Friesen (1992) and later by Young, Friesen and Borycki (1994) that suggests that there is a relationship between social support and educational attainment. An important direction for research is for a call for more work on family interaction patterns. New studies suggest that these may even be related to the establishment of career identity (Lopez, 1989; Penick

& Jepson, 1992). Penick and Jepson (1992) add that there should be a greater body of research in this direction.

But there remains a substantial amount of controversy in understanding what variables in the family affect what outcomes in the career decision making and eventual job satisfaction process. Empirical contributions sometimes lend fodder rather than light to the controversy. The availability of so many influencing variables makes data analysis a herculean task.

Chapter 3

Cultural Diversity and Family Influence

"Community cannot for long feed on itself; it can only flourish with the coming of others from beyond..."
Howard Thurman

Ethnicity, class, and culture regularly interface with the world of work. Many immigrants and families of color take a substantially different point of view in the career decision making process than those families who feel positioned with maneuverability and privilege. Sometimes family conflicts emerge. Children don't necessarily want to follow the suggestions of their parents, but cultural mores demand that they not disobey them. These issues are considered in this chapter. A template of ideas is presented for counselors to use when exploring multicultural family influence. Included among these ideas are demographics, acculturation and enculturation, language, religion, and attitudes about work.

How a family influences the career decision making and planning of its members will, for the most part, be related to culturally specific factors that are assumed to be as meaningful. Exploring the interaction between cultural diversity and family influence helps us to understand the uniqueness of all clients and the cultures from which they arose. Everyone comes from his/her own individually different culture, lifestyle, and context. Race, class, and culture play a substantial role in how the world is perceived in the family, especially the world of work, as several illustrations will suggest. In this chapter, we will use specific examples of recent immigrants, established families, and selected ethnic groups. Although this chapter will take a generic approach to the discussion of cultural diversity and family influence, without question, all cultures are different and there needs to be a culturally specific understanding of family influence as well.

Cultural Changes in the United States

Since the Vietnam War era, the composition of the population of the United States has been witness to a dramatic shift in its mixture of multiracial, multiethnic, and multiple language groups. The transitioning citizenry has led to the creation of a patchwork of cultural pluralism. The rapidly changing demographics, continuing immigration, and the globalization of work have impacted the cultural frame of reference that people and families have used to view the world.

Individual and cultural identities which have been more clearly pointed out in the past are also diverging with each new generation. The identification of a culture or ethnicity referred to by a somewhat foggy designation like "Hispanic," "Asian," "African American," "Pacific Islander" has been made even more convoluted through both the recent trend toward intermarriage and the adoption of new identities in a new country by immigrants. The broadly stroked term, ALANA (African-American, Latina/Latin, Asian-Pacific Islander American, Native American), is now frequently and colloquially used to group together people of color and their contrasts with Caucasians on a variety of different variables.

Assimilation

Cultural assimilation has resulted in word usage reflecting new cultural identities. Words like "Hispanic" used by first generation immigrants can become "Hispanic-American" for the next generation. And in this second generation there can be a departure in identity from "Hispanic-American" identified to "American" identified. At San Francisco State University, for instance, Asian students might be characterized as "Asian," "Asian-American" but Asian identified, or "Asian-American" but American identified, depending upon how the student experiences cultural and familial assimilation. There's an often reported continuum between acculturation (the incorporation of the norms and values of the dominant society and enculturation) and retaining the norms and values of the indigenous country.

This can be made more intriguing when words like Hispanic and Asian are given greater specificity. Hispanics can be Mexican, South American, Caribbean, Iberian, or Central American among others. Asians on the other hand can be Chinese, Japanese, North or South Korean, Filipino, Vietnamese, or South Asian, including Indian. Ultimately, the assumptions about the world and familial biases and attitudes shift as people become more intertwined with individuals from other cultures.

So, summarizing multicultural family influences on career development is a demanding task.

Workforce Changes

The workforce is changing as well. The working populace in the United States, which was once predominantly male and Caucasian, has now become enriched with large increases in women and people of color. Greater workplace opportunities have certainly arisen for a multiethnic, multicultural workforce partly due to interventions by Federal and State legislatures with trade agreements and to an increase in the numbers of technically trained immigrants. Civil rights and liberties have also transformed the workforce, in part, with legislative efforts like Title VII of the Civil Rights Act of 1964 resulting in greater opportunities in the workplace for women and people of color. Still, in spite of these well intentioned efforts, the majority of the many different multiethnic and diversified groups remain, for the most part, worse off economically than their Caucasian peers.

Immigrants have been recently documented as playing a significant role in the changing demographics of the nation's educational system and workforce. A majority of the entering class at the University of California at Berkeley in the Fall of 2002, had one parent who was born outside of the United States (Schevitz, 2002). At the private Jesuit University of San Francisco (USF) in 2004, 60% of the students identified themselves as members of "minority" groups; 38% were the first members of their respective families to attend college. According to the USF president, Dr. Stephen Privett, S.J., the families of 25% of the undergraduates speak native languages other than English. The undergraduate college at USF is the 16th most ethnically diverse in the United States (Nolte, 2004). In California, people of color now represent a majority of the population.

Multicultural Career Counseling

With these changing demographics, organizations like the American Counseling Association (ACA) and specifically its largest division, the National Career Development Association (NCDA), have focused upon the need for professionals to have awareness, knowledge, and skills to work with an increasingly diversified population. Indeed, an entire section of the career counseling competencies of the NCDA (1997) is devoted to working with diverse populations. Titled "Diverse Populations," the competencies in the section suggest that career counselors demonstrate they can identify needs that are unique to diverse populations. Further, career counselors must develop the ability to accommodate the needs of these diverse groups. Counselors should be able to ensure effective communication, identify alternative counseling approaches when necessary, have knowledge of community referral sources, assist others in understanding the unique needs of various groups, design appropriate programs for hard to serve people, and advocate for the career development and employment opportunities of diverse populations.

Thus, there is professional encouragement to incorporate ethnic information in our study of family influence. The NCDA competencies call for new approaches that can assist the needs of a changing population. While career development theories in the United States have been largely positivistic and focused upon the individual, the emerging multicultural workforce and population has a worldview that may not completely fit the framework of these theories. New career development approaches need to be developed and utilized that are less Eurocentric and, instead, focus upon the uniqueness of different cultures and the variability within cultures.

In exploring the influences of multiethnic and multicultural families, there is a need to examine both the universal characteristics that everyone experiences as being part of a family and the culture-specific experiences. Multicultural counseling is referred to by many as the fourth force in counseling theory. As we shall see, the cultural context of career development for a family of color is vastly different from the context that is discussed in traditional career development theory. The diminishment of employment opportunities, discrimination, and denial from equal educational opportunities have been discussed at length in other sources. Family history and context play vivid roles in how information is passed from generation to generation including helping the next generation to prepare for available job opportunities.

Career Reconstruction

In counseling all clients, one variable that is generally not considered is the phenomenon of career reconstruction, the need to give up a previous career choice to take a different career path. This term has been used in the past when people have a trade that is no longer needed by society and they must reconstruct their careers. Milk wagon drivers and keypunch operators come to mind as careers that are no longer needed. And career reconstruction is a term that can also be used when individuals are forced to give up a particular dream or fantasy of what their career could be like. Actors, writers, musicians, rock star wannabes all exemplify people who may need to reconstruct their career because they can't earn a living doing what they were trained to do. Career reconstruction affects children and other family members because the parents may be conflicted about the careers they have to assume. The creation of a new career when there is no possibility of using one's past experience or education to begin a career or continue to perform previously understood job tasks is emotionally demanding for everyone.

Richard—A Case of Discrimination

When Richard received his medical degree, he was among the top scholars in his class. His father was a bus driver and, from the day Richard was born, his father told him that one day he would become a great heart surgeon. Richard's hope was to pursue cardiology and practice medicine as a cardiovascular surgeon. But, when he described his career goals to the faculty and hospital chiefs of staff during medical school, Richard was discouraged from this specialization. He was told that since he happened to be African-American, he would have a difficult time practicing medicine in this specialty area because patients would not want a heart surgeon who was African-American. Richard prevailed anyway, completed his internship and residencies, and then took on additional cardiology and surgical residencies. When he finished all of his training, he passed his boards with extraordinary high marks. But, when he went to pursue professional medical practice, he found that the opportunities that he expected to be available were not. He couldn't join the type of medical practice that he expected and had to opt for a different type of practice and lifestyle. Discouraged that he wouldn't be able to practice in the way that he expected, he became more involved in academic medicine and research. While he has had a career as a medical school professor and surgical expert, he was never able to practice privately in the manner in which he dreamed. He had to reconstruct his career. In spite of his family preparation, he never overcame his emotional disappointment.

Alan—A Musician or a Lawyer?

Alan was a musician for 13 years. He had an Ivy League education and law school degree. His father was a lawyer who wanted him to join the firm. He took the bar exam in Florida. But, instead of using his education to join his father in legal practice, Alan wanted to pursue a career as a singer with his own band. Some might describe him as a privileged idealist, but this was his desire. So, after completing law school, he formed a duo and took off on the road. The two musicians wrote their own words and lyrics and made a moderate living playing in small clubs and different colleges and universities for over a decade. While they had their own cult following, they never reached the popularity they dreamed of. In their late thirties and with children to support, they decided that enough was enough and Alan would need to come in from the cold and get a real job. So, in mid life he reconstructed his career, dusted off his bar license, and began working as a criminal prosecutor in a county district attorney's office. Interestingly, his teenage son has become a musician.

While Alan's story demonstrates the nature of career reconstruction and its disappointments, his at least had a positive ending, as he was able to earn more income as a lawyer than as a musician. However, most reconstructed careers usually result in downward mobility resulting in a continuing experience of psychological stress. A professor of physics in a former homeland may be working in a downtown restaurant, earning many times what was earned in the mother country, but not having the prestige or relative income in comparison to other Americans. Richard's experience in contrast to Alan's illustrates this point. It is not dissimilar to the experiences that other people of color have had, particularly immigrants.

So, when exploring the influence of immigrant and multiethnic parents on the career decisions of their children, different factors emerge that never need to be considered by children who have parents or relatives that are more a part of the established mainstream of America.

Immigrants—Career Reconstruction and Assimilation

The degree to which immigrants develop satisfaction with their careers is often dictated by the bilateral enculturation-acculturation process. And there are many significant sources of stress to which immigrant families must respond (Chope & Fang, 1999). These include, but are not limited to, the following:

Physical Stress: Immigrants must adjust to a new, unfamiliar physical environment with different housing standards and climate. For children, this may be frightening.

Biological Stress: Immigrants may need to change their diet. Foods, familiar in the homeland may not exist in the newly adopted country. Changing the diet can affect the immigrant's sense of security and identity.

Social Stress: Immigrants will be affected by vast changes in employment opportunities, educational instruction, and ethnic and social status. They may "cocoon" themselves, unwilling to venture into unfamiliar territories. They may find that their indigenous values are compromised. The role models that children will have become represented by parents who restrict them in their adventures outside the family. Risk taking will be frowned upon and drawing attention to the family will be discouraged.

Cultural Stress: Immigrants will encounter new politics, language, religion, and purchasing power. There will be a greater variety of choices available than in the homeland. They will have a whole new learning curve.

Psychological Stress: Immigrants may have their values, beliefs, attitudes, and "sense of belonging" changed. They will have a difficult time feeling that they are not outsiders. The children may be overly protected and persuaded to listen to the parents when making career and educational choices.

Adjustment to work for many immigrant families and families of color has demanded career reconstruction. For them, life in the new country may not be what many had anticipated. The identity conflicts are unimaginable. There is a quagmire of vocational and cultural issues as they move from feeling pleased about being in a politically stable country to being depressed about not measuring up to their career dreams and expectations.

The movie *House of Sand and Fog* directed by Vadim Perelman illustrates these conflicts nicely, however dramatically, and exemplifies the career reconstruction that many immigrants face. In the film, an Iranian immigrant, Behrani (aptly portrayed by Ben Kingsley), has to reconstruct his career and his life after being forced from his homeland. He had apparently held a high military position in the long deposed government of the Shah. The film demonstrates the struggles of immigrants as Behrani and his family try to maintain pride and cultural identity against a backdrop of humiliation and discrimination. They experience the dilemmas of enculturation-acculturation and the stressors enumerated above.

So, understanding immigrants and others who have been disenfranchised forces counselors to provide services that are sensitive to these issues. In studying families of immigrants, the work patterns in the former country may be quite different from those in the new country. And that new work may be reconstructed work.

The Influence of Social and Political Changes

The influence of families in the career development process of immigrants and people of color is complex for other reasons as well. Dramatic changes of a social and political nature affect career choice and opportunity (Chope & Fang, 1999). Traditional patterns of social relations that espouse filial piety and respect for elders in the past are not necessarily taken into account by younger generations. The more traditionally accepted belief in many cultures of moral development and knowledge fulfillment has been replaced by a desire for quick material benefits through speculation and the pursuit of new economic opportunities. The dot com boom helped to spur this along.

In Hong Kong and Taiwan, for example, older generations preserve traditional values while the younger generation rejects conservatism and tradition. Younger Asian immigrants are seen to crave autonomy, self expression, self-assertion, and individually-oriented achievement (Lee, 1983).

When Chinese immigrants seek career counseling, they can't be attended to as simply third or fourth generation Chinese-Americans. They may have different values and have witnessed the evolution of their own parents needing to reconstruct their careers. They may be attentive to growing opportunities in fields that are not those that are understood or supported by their parents.

How the Multicultural Family Worldview Affects Caucasians

The increased focus upon cultural diversity has had a serendipitous effect on how Caucasians view their own identity and pertinent career and cultural development. While Helms (1995) has drawn attention to this for years, there has still not been a driving focus on the complexity of issues and cultural attitudes that encompass being Caucasian and American. As we focus upon families and career development, this is also a time to continue to understand some of the elaborate amalgamations in the variety of cultures that make up Caucasian-Americans.

Approaching Your Own Multiculturalism Through the Study of Family

Appearance isn't everything. I know that in my own experience, with an increasing focus upon multiculturalism, I became annoyed that I was always classified as "white" or Caucasian since my family was identified as predominantly Western European. People had biases about me because of what they perceived my upbringing to be. Unless they had seen my children, they would never had known that I had been in a multicultural relationship. But with the increasing emphasis on multiculturalism in all academic aspects of service provision, I became more interested in my own "diversity." With the helpfulness of some of my cousins and the high speed technology of the Internet to search out genealogical patterns, I was able to shift my point of view about myself and my family as I discovered and studied the family cultures from which I came.

I have learned that I am not distinctively European. In fact, I'm mostly Celtic. The ancestors of my maternal grandparents are Irish and German. My German ancestors were also partly Jewish; my great grandmother was Jewish, a fact that was discovered only recently, having never been discussed by my own parents. My fraternal grandparents were Scottish and British. My Scottish clan was Crawford, which happens to be my middle name. None of this was known by me until I did my search. But I feel enriched by the process and am able, as a Caucasian man, to experience the complexity of my own multiculturalism.

Celtic and German cultures are as different as they can be, obviously with different histories and languages. Even the Irish, Scottish, and British represent distinctive cultures. And while they all speak English, the dialects and word use have clear individual differences.

My family history is made up of salesmen, ship captains, and carriage builders, all Celtic and Germanic occupations and all individualistic as opposed to collectivistic in social orientation. My father was a factory worker at the Ford Motor Company until he moved into an office position, serving as a personnel manager at Ford Motor. He spent his entire life in the automobile industry, retiring as a manager of human relations. His interest in people is related to mine. But his passion was art, which he never pursued because he didn't think it would allow him to have the lifestyle he wanted. My sister inherited those skills, and today she flourishes as a commercial artist.

Changing Demographics Demand a Reconfiguring of Career Theories

As pointed out by many (Niles & Harris-Bowlsbey, 2002), while there has been distinctive growth in the increase in opportunities for people of color, people with disabilities, women, and gays, lesbians, bisexuals and transgenders, there continue to be serious roadblocks, in some cases leading to large unemployment for groups of people like young African-American men. Other people of color may be employed in service oriented positions that provide little opportunity for growth and are typically providing employment with minimum wages and few, if any, benefits like health and dental care. The impact of variables like discrimination, limited economic opportunity, poor career development, and the lack of familial models of successful career choices, has led to a greater degree of focus on contextual variables in career planning.

An Emphasis on Context

For the past twenty years, many practitioners have been dissatisfied with career development theories that did not take into consideration contextual variables like economic opportunity and discrimination to allow for approaches that would assist people who were raised in circumstances very different from those upon which the majority of career development strategies were proposed. Accordingly, the last few years have foreseen an attempt by career development theorists and professionals to develop new approaches that give more credence to understanding the context and manner in which people are raised and how that affects career development (Blustein, 1997; Kim, Atkinson, & Umemoto, 2001). Quite clearly, career decision making needs to be studied in the context of newer conceptual frameworks and theories that may be more useful than the older theories of "test 'em and tell 'em." These newer theories are promoted in major academic texts like Niles and Harris-Bowlsbey (2002) and Gysbers, Heppner, and Johnston (2003). Postmodern approaches as articulated by Niles and Harris-Bowlsbey include creating narratives, contextualizing career development and utilizing constructivism, stemming from the seminal work of George Kelly (1955), to give greater meaning to the career decision making process.

Individualism Versus Collectivism

The more western European approaches that Gysbers et al. (2003) describe as tenets may no longer be accurate portrayals of the current work world in the United States. For example, individualism and autonomy are becoming overshadowed by feelings of collectivism that stem from the family and culture of people of color. Collectivists believe that the interests of the group rather than the individual should be advocated for and being part of a group effort is more valuable than individual effort. Affluence, seen by many as distinctively American, may not have as much impact among those who are more concerned with helping people in their own cultures and practicing in a manner that reflects values more related to social justice.

Nonlinear Career Paths

In addition, as I have pointed out earlier (Chope, 2000), the work world is not the linear world that has been experienced by many up until the dot com boom. Now there's a greater call toward viewing the world of work more like a matrix; people can create some element of opportunity by maneuvering through a mobilized system rather than waiting to climb a company ladder or break through a class ceiling. This approach fits in with the thinking of people from cultures who also don't necessarily envision a linear career path. Some cultures place a greater degree of emphasis on interconnections, and career paths may be more cyclical than linear. Cultures that have more focus upon agriculture are particularly sensitive to the cyclical nature of work that doesn't progress in a linear manner.

Curiously, companies are taking some of this orientation into their own consciousness as they move from stable career patterns to patterns that reflect projects and project-driven growth. People may not be hired for extended periods of time, but rather may be asked to do a project.

These workplace changes will, however, be disruptive to the career deployment of people who think that careers move in a linear fashion. In cultures where the expectation is that hard work and advancement will lead to progressive increases in salaries, there will be unfortunate disappointments. People from cultures which have a greater sense of ease about work disruptions will be more enthusiastic about project-driven employment.

Work May Be Losing Its Centrality

Work may not be as central to people's lives as many have believed in the past. People of color may gravitate to family, community, and spirituality with greater comfort than the work world. In addition, the pernicious aspects of discrimination and the lack of opportunities for many in mainstream culture make the importance of work less of a focus. Family obligations and the creation of a work and life balance take on greater degrees of importance for many people of color in contrast to mainstream Americans. In many cultures, there is the expectation that sacrifices should be made for the family, but not necessarily for the employer.

Using Narratives

A popular device for counselors to deploy in gathering information about the career choices of people of color as well as those with reconstructed or nonlinear career paths is the narrative. Many cultures appreciate oral histories and narratives over the written word.

The narrative approach to career counseling is a type of storytelling that can be likened to an individual or family oral history. Cochran (1997) has pointed out that narratives in career counseling can help clients to gain a sense of the past history, current circumstances, and potential future goals. There is also the possibility for expansion upon the future goals because the story continues to be written. In addition, the narrative can have an integrating impact on a person's sense of who they are in the work world. Sometimes this can be done in a written fashion and sometimes it can be done with lifelines that demarcate critical events in a person's life. In addition, the narrative allows a person to create a story that has whatever ending he or she wants.

I have covered this earlier (Chope, 2000). Career decisions can unfold like a good story and make for a pretty good drama. None of these stories needs to be long but with a little prodding about the family, the tale can be pretty interesting. I've devised a little four sentence exercise that has allowed people to write their stories as part of a homework lesson. You can try this yourself or suggest that a client use the four sentence structure. This is an attempt to have people write a story in four short sentences. And it can be the beginning of the narrative that incorporates family and culture.

The sentences go like this:

> It all began, so we are told, when...
> And then...
> So...
> And finally...

The career story can not only help to define your own aspirations and interests, it can also structure a meaningful reflection on the manner in which your family influenced your career decision. Expanding on the story is certainly useful information for any counselor to have to create a more in-depth counseling experience. Look at the following example from my client Pacho and then try the exercise yourself.

Pacho. Pacho wrote the following brief narrative as a homework assignment that was a part of his career counseling. "It all began, so we are told, when papa said that in America I would not really amount to anything so I would need to get some work right away so that I could support myself and the family and any babies I might have. And then, after I got upset about being in America, I decided that I would get a permanent job in a canning factory that no one could take away from me. So, I joined a local cannery and stayed on that job for 17 years, unhappy most of the time. And finally, the cannery was closed and the company moved to South America and I wasn't willing to go back there with them. So I had to decide what to do and that is why I'm getting counseling. Maybe I can go to school now and do things differently. My father was wrong. I could have done this differently and not spent so long in the factory."

The career story helps people to create their sense of identity. The story can be expanded upon regularly like in a journal or in the presence of a counselor. The characters in the author's life, the protagonists and antagonists, can be described in any way that the author likes. The story can be used to gather information that can be used to complete a template regarding the issues and attitudes that different people have about work and relationships that have been influenced by their cultures.

Types of Information to Understand Family Influence in Multicultural Career Counseling

In the postmodern approaches to career counseling, Niles and Harris-Bowlsbey (2002, p. 89) point to a greater concern for being aware of the contextual factors that are a part of the career counseling process. This is especially important in work with a multicultural population. Level of acculturation, family values, cultural heritage as well as economic issues, histories of discrimination, and unusual work opportunities can be incorporated into the career counseling process. The contextual focus of some writers (Young, Valach, & Collin, 1996) has begun to point out that information about the theoretical and more positivistic approaches has been giving way to an orientation that is more eclectic and integrative. A changing focus on context has allowed counselors to become less dogmatic as they embrace the complexity of work in multiculturalism that earlier theories and perspectives did not focus upon. Change and stability, the organizing principles of career development, will be moderated by the developmental path and interpersonal and cultural contexts in which an individual experiences work.

There is a template of ideas that counselors can use when they explore the influence of family from any culture. This information aids the alliance between the client and the counselor relative to the goals of the counseling, the tasks involved, and the bond that results when two work together to achieve common goals (Bordin, 1979). Counselors should be able to gather information on the following: the demographic environment, presence of subcultures, legal status, acculturation/ enculturation, language, religion, attitudes about work, rules in the family system, and gender stereotypes.

Demographic Environment

First, of course, is to understand the nature of the population in the area that the client resides and how representative it is of the client's culture. This will require a bit of background work and some information about demographics in your area. Some of this work should be done before the first meeting. The knowledge base can help the counselor to avoid stereotypes and create an atmosphere where the client feels some degree of acceptance. Information about typical career paths of people from different ethnic groups will be useful in order to confront some of the attitudes that clients will have about engaging in activities that are unfamiliar to the family. The information can help to provide appropriate suggestions for activities that will not appear to be disrespectful. Knowledge of a particular culture will also create an element of caring and acceptance, enabling the client to consider returning for additional sessions. The underutilization of career services by people of color is well documented (Flores & Heppner, 2002).

Presence of Subcultures

It is also of paramount importance that the counselor understand any of the subcultures that exist within a culture. For example, the broad categorization of "Latin" or "Hispanic" really needs to be broken down further into knowing the cultural differences between South American, Central American, Iberian, Cuban, Caribbean, Mexican and other cultures.

Likewise, Middle Eastern ethnic groups share many similarities in culture and traditions which include the importance of family, spirituality, and a collectivistic set of societal expectations. But they also have many differences including language (e.g., Arabic, Persian, Farsi, Iraqi, Armenian) as well as differences in religion (e.g., Christianity, Judaism, and Islam). Clearly, each of these subcultures can have different language idioms, religious beliefs, and family attitudes about work and position. The family attitudes and traditions in these more microscopic cultures will all be different and need to be understood in order for the client to be willing to become more revealing.

Legal Status

In addition, for new immigrants there should be some information available on whether the client's family's values and traditions are documented. It is within this context that the use of a narrative or storytelling approach can be most beneficial. Further, there should be some discussion of the generational differences within the family. For example, is the client a first, second, or third generation immigrant? Does the client feel assimilated or acculturated or enculturated?

Acculturation/Enculturation

Knowing how clients feel about their culture is important in order to understand the clients' cultural adaptation process. Different clients will be ashamed or proud of their culture. Many will wish to remain separate from their own ethnic group. And, in more complex examples, some will wish to adopt the values of the new culture while maintaining a hold on other values from the indigenous culture. For example, a client may incorporate the work values of American companies while continuing to uphold the family values of the indigenous culture. Some others may feel individualistic at work, but collectivistic in assisting their community.

Language

Language is an important source of identity for people from different cultures. The language that the client uses at home may contrast with that which is used at work or in school. A sense of identity is developed with the use of language, and it can reflect the dualism of acculturation/enculturation. The dialect of language may be important, and clients can express how a particular dialect represents a further capturing of their identity.

Religion

Religion and religious values may play an important role in the career choices of many. In the United States, a Protestant work ethic drives much of the economy. This ethic is often seen as antiwomen and anti-immigrant; and there has been criticism of its limited multicultural applicability. Curiously, there is a current interest in the role of spirituality in the workplace. In some companies, individuals are allowed to have religious experiences during breaks at their offices and factories.

But any person who follows a nonmainstream religion may feel uncomfortable on the job. Jewish workers, for example, for years felt that they couldn't ask for time off during the High Holy Days and Yom Kippur. Quite a splash was made in the 1960s when Dodger pitcher Sandy Koufax informed his teammates that he was not going to pitch in a World Series game if the date of the game was on Yom Kippur. While some adjustments have reflected sensitivity to Jews in the workforce, there continues to be a need for sensitivity to the religious values of many others like Sikhs, Muslims, Hindus, and Buddhists, to name a few of the many living religions.

Attitudes About Work

Some families just want the children to earn money and be independent. Others want their children to achieve. And still others want their children to refrain from drawing attention to themselves. The following list will be responded to differently by people from different cultures. But it will be useful to add to information about the worldview of the family and culture regarding work.

Exercise

Describe how your family feels about the following work-related attributes:

Be competitive and try to be a standout at whatever you do.

Be proactive in your work; aggressively try to predict what your employer wants next.

Take appropriate risks at work, like speaking your mind about job-related tasks.

Be decisive, committed, confident, and steadfast.

Have a sense of urgency about your job tasks and accomplish more than is asked for.

Be autocratic and not democratic in your relationships with coworkers and people who report to you.

Other attitudes about work can also be related to earnings. Family attitudes about money, savings, assets of friends, dollar stretching, asset equity, supportive loans from others, institutional loans, venture money, and the trustworthiness of financial institutions can speak volumes about how people have assimilated into the mainstream American culture.

Rules in the Family System

The family may have different rules about the power and the influence of the extended family. Grandparents, aunts, cousins, and uncles may have a role regarding career selection and education that is different from that in other cultures. There may be certain demands on the manner in which elders are to be respected. In many cultures, elders are held with reverence and respect. Confronting or disagreeing with parents can be seen as a sign of disrespect. And this can have quite a negative impact on a person who is looking for guidance from an elder family member but doesn't necessarily want to accept the advice. That is a sign of going against the wishes of the elder and is characterized as disrespectful.

There can also be issues of what will bring shame upon the family. And there may be conflicts in the family over just fitting in rather than being "Americanized." There is a lot of pressure to conform to both the norms of the family as well as the norms of the culture. But the reputation of the family is a primary concern. Refraining from shaming the family is also a primary attribute of many cultures. Most clients may find that majoring in programs that the family doesn't approve of, failing to achieve academically, and not being professionally successful are among the variables that the family uses to judge the children.

Many immigrant families and families of color take a substantially more rigid point of view in the career decision making processes of their children than those families who happen to feel that they have more maneuverability and privilege. Accordingly, more culturally diversified families try to protect their children by demanding that they follow familial instructions about what educational and career goals to pursue. Further, the children, as an extension of the family, are the next generation to bring pride to the family. In many cultures, when the children are unsuccessful, the family feels that shame has been brought upon them.

As an advisor at San Francisco State University, I have been informed by many students of color that they don't necessarily wish to follow the suggestions of their parents, but their cultural mores demand that they not disobey their family elders. So, they may attend schools that represent the choices of their parents, major in programs they are indifferent to, and enter career fields with which they have few interests. This can be further complicated if the children continue to live in the family home as adults.

Background data like these have served to lead to an increased emphasis on the importance of multicultural understanding and development in the career counseling field. Several cases help to illustrate the point.

Nazara

Nazara was a client with a rich Middle Eastern tradition. Her family had emigrated from Afghanistan and was safely ensconced in the city of Fremont, California, a popular city for South Asians in the San Francisco Bay Area. She was planning on majoring in accounting and helping her family business. As the eldest, she carried a banner for the family. There were high expectations for her, to some extent, unrealistically high. But her parents had been through several wars and the occupation of their homeland, so she felt that she should do her duty and contribute to the family's legacy and its well-being. The career goal for her was to enter some form of business after finishing an undergraduate degree in business administration.

Nazara, however, ran into a problem with her accounting classes and after three tries was unable to pass them. Consequently she was not able to matriculate in business administration and achieve a college degree in the area. Seemingly this was not a problem. However, her family had already told other family members in the United States and in Afghanistan that Nazara would be receiving a business degree. Further, it was assumed that Nazara would not only help her parents and two siblings, but that she would also be in a position to help other family members emigrate to the United States and set up their own businesses as well.

Nazara came to career counseling because she needed to select a new major and she requested help in approaching her family to tell them that she was not going to receive a business degree after all. The counselor was able to point out to Nazara that there were many ways to enter business and that she did not necessarily need a business degree in order to succeed. The business degree idea came from her father who thought that people went to American colleges in order to learn how to generate more money. The counselor advised her to consider a variety of liberal arts classes. That would give her the foundation to pursue opportunities in fields like human relations and corporate communications, thus avoiding finance and accounting. While she had a difficult time explaining the counselor's ideas to her parents, she was nevertheless supported by them in her decision.

Kim: A Third Generation Korean Immigrant

For most of her life, Kim had worked in the family dry cleaning and laundry business. At the University of California, Berkeley, she wanted to major in art and consider going on for advanced degrees in sculpture. The family had other ideas. Her father had been a well known soccer player in Korea and when he immigrated into the United States, he said he had to give that all up and take care of his wife and two daughters. Now he expected his daughters to help with the family business. He wanted Kim to major in business or accounting so that she could join the dry cleaning business and help to expand it. Kim had no interest in business or being a part of the family enterprise. Since she wouldn't major in business, her father said that he wouldn't support her going to Cal-Berkeley and that she would have to finance her education herself. She was able to afford her education by securing loans and transferring to San Francisco State and pursuing art and sculpture.

Both Nazara and Kim were going against the wishes of their respective families and felt that they were bringing shame to their homes. Moreover, they both needed career and psychological counseling for the emotional turmoil that they were experiencing. But this too was a problem because in their cultures the belief was that the family should be used in discussing personal problems. Both families felt that psychological problems demonstrated signs of weakness. Mental health problems only brought shame to the family. Counselors must be sensitive to all of these issues and appreciate the strength of the messages from the client's family.

Gender Stereotypes

The culture can also have gender stereotypes regarding the roles that men and women play relative to work, educational experiences, and family responsibilities. Relationship status is also influenced by the culture and the family. In a family of creation, the attitudes that partners have toward each other will often be influenced by the stereotypes that have been inculcated by the family and culture over a period of years.

Career counselors should be aware of the differential expectations regarding appropriateness of jobs for each gender that affect the kinds of jobs young men and women prepare for and select. Counselors should also be knowledgeable of how partners or husbands and wives are able to accommodate themselves to each other's careers. A most interesting question is how a woman's success affects the relationship. There are undoubtedly cultural differences in expectations about parenting roles. And the way pregnant women are viewed and treated will differ from culture to culture.

Freddy

As described in a case study (Consoli & Chope, 2005), my client Freddy experienced a great deal of tension in his relationship with his wife. He was a first generation Mexican-American who had married a second generation Mexican-American named Vera. He felt that some of his employment problems were directly related to differences he experienced with his wife. His world-view was collectivistic, hers was more individualistic and influenced by her assimilation into the culture of the United States. He wanted a tightly knit family because he believed that relationships with the family of origin were central to his identity. Vera was more focused upon individual autonomy and she enjoyed making plans, with an orientation on the future. Freddy, on the other hand, was more centered on the present or "here and now." Vera had hoped to have a home, children and a lifestyle that was a reflection of her perceptions of success in the United States. And she had hoped to travel while he wanted to spend his vacations closer to home with his family of origin and any children they may have.

There were other differences between them. Vera had grown up in a lower middle class household in the San Francisco Bay Area, and she had hoped to have a lifestyle that was a clear upgrade from the one she had originated from. So, she pushed herself and Freddy into work that was not necessarily meaningful, but instead paid well even if it required long hours. Freddy just wanted to have steady work. Moreover, and to the chagrin of Vera, Freddy wanted steady income and did not feel as entrepreneurial as Vera did. In addition, he wanted to help to support his mother who was a domestic helper as well as his sister who worked as a hair stylist. He felt that the resources of his family should be parceled out. Vera was against this, feeling that Freddy was enabling the family to support a lifestyle that didn't represent the hard efforts that she had to put out. Freddy felt that he was just maintaining their health and well being. Freddy found it difficult to communicate with Vera about these issues, compounding the career work, and leading to his suffering panic attacks and symptoms of agoraphobia.

Freddy's case shows a conflict in many of the tenets described earlier where there are disagreements between family members that reflect the differences between the older and newer tenets of career decision making.

Chapter Summary

This chapter has provided a variety of illustrations and case examples on career decision making with respect to culturally specific factors.

Exploring cultural diversity and family influence allows for a deeper appreciation of the uniqueness of all clients and the cultures they came from. Being aware of differential pressures on people and their responses to them, like career reconstruction, adds to the essential knowledge and awareness that all career counselors need to become increasingly sensitive and effective. A template was presented for career counselors to use when gathering information from a multicultural clientele.

Chapter 4

How to Gather Data to Assess Family Influence

"It is better to know some of the questions than to know all of the answers."
James Thurber

In data collection, it's most important to be consistent and systematic. This chapter offers a variety of methods to ensure that this takes place. Several different protocols will be offered along with an approach called the family genogram. A final newly developed protocol will be presented that may prove to be the most useful of these. In addition to a systematic list of questions, this protocol, unlike the others, offers ideas for in-depth follow up to the original questions. The ensuing material provides a discussion of the kinds of answers the questions elicit and how to evaluate them.

Assessing the influence of the family in career decision making is quite demanding for a variety of reasons. The dearth of standardized instruments for data collection is the first challenge. Additionally, many standardized instruments that are currently available hardly take into account the massive restructuring of today's families. With the exception of some instruments like the *Family Environment Scale* (Moos & Moos, 1981) or *Career Factors Inventory* (Chartrand, Robbins, & Morrill, 1997), there really aren't any easily available standardized instruments that can measure family influence.

The *Family Environment Scale* can help to measure the social and environmental characteristics of families and may be useful in conceptualizing family cohesion and conflict along with the achievement orientation, among seven other scales. The *Career Factors Inventory* measures informational and emotional factors that can lead to career indecision, factors that are also vulnerable to family influences.

Simply asking clients to reflect upon which family members under what circumstances were most influential in their career and educational decisions may, in the end, generate only superficial responses. But most standardized quantitative instruments used to assist in the data gathering process are less than perfect.

Qualitative measures seem to be used most frequently. Some researchers have been known to use Q-sorts to explore major influences in career decision making, but these haven't been arranged in a format that can be easily used by a counselor. And many counselors and coaches will use the genogram as a qualitative instrument that can be completed at home by the client or in the office with the help of a counselor. This will be discussed in more depth in this chapter.

For the most part, counselors and researchers assess family influence through the use of retrospective questionnaires. While this process is systematic, it isn't standardized. These instruments reflect a potpourri of ideas that counselors and researchers, myself included, have produced for determining which facts are the most relevant for clients and counselors to use for assessment purposes.

Today's Families Are Really Quite Complex

In addition to the problems with instruments, assessing family influence can be complicated by the vast array of variables presented by the modern family of origin. These variables can include the immediate and extended family and the contextual variables of birth order, family socioeconomic status, educational levels of family members, and anticipated educational, vocational, and economic levels of the children (Bratcher, 1982; Ulrich & Dunne, 1986).

Just as we're beginning to incorporate information on the influence of the family in career counseling, the population of the United States is undergoing revolutionary changes in the structure of the family. Along with these changes, some of the current work patterns and lifestyles practiced by 21st century families no longer resemble many of the more traditional patterns of work. Job shifts exemplified by portfolio careers with multiple income streams, home based work, telecommuting, and dual worker/career families are a few of the emerging patterns, although dual earner families have become commonplace over the last two decades.

Accompanying these substantial changes are shifts in the structure of the family. There have been large increases in the number of gay, lesbian, bisexual, and transgender (GLBT) families. Domestic partnerships are slowly being legally recognized in many work venues; in a few cities, there are moves to legalize gay marriages, while many states try to block them.

Single adults, both gay and heterosexual, are raising children in record numbers. The United States Bureau of Census (1994) reports that 22.3 % of all families with minor children are single parent families. Moreover, close to 80% of these households are run solely by women. A lack of available social support for single parents often puts a strain on extended family members as well. In some cases, the extended family members take over child rearing responsibilities.

Grandparents, especially among multicultural families, have become primary care providers in numerous urban settings. And more than a few parents are raising children in their second and third marriage or relationship. Stepfamilies are common and stepparents can have a significant impact, both positive and negative, on the career and educational plans of their stepchildren.

The Changing Workplace

There's an immense amount of instability in the workplace. In California and other parts of the country "dot coms" have become "dot bombs" and turned into "dot compost." Now, perspective employees try to enter work places that are characterized as "not com." The economic recovery of 2004 appears to be "jobless" (Peterson & Gonzales, 2005). And while there is economic expansion, there is not necessarily employment expansion. With the globalization of the job market, this unsettling trend may not just be temporary. While instability may increase the choices that people have available to them, it also lights the fires of fear.

Even the concept of "career" is in some jeopardy as portfolio careers and project driven work become increasingly commonplace. Futurist Bill Bridges (1995) predicts that in the place of jobs, there will be "part-time and temporary work situations" (p.1). Likewise, some workers currently choose to have more than one job or source of income. And, while one of these income streams may be related to their interests and skills, another stream may be used simply to provide income, independent of concern over developing a career path. There simply aren't many families that have the luxury of a single income household with adequate benefits like health insurance.

Some part-time jobs pay reasonably well and are described as "mindless," allowing an income provider the opportunity to focus upon another more important career track while ensuring income stability for the family. Students of all majors and persuasions, along with people who pursue work in the creative and the performing arts, know all too well that multiple income streams can be a way of life, at least for part of a person's career. Others, like me, will create multiple income streams as a hedge against economic disruption. While I work as a full-time college professor, I'm able to generate other sources of income. I can secure grants, teach in the summer school, write books, give speeches, and consult with people and organizations in my private practice.

Today, people growing up and making career decisions live in a world where there is a dramatic increase in the numbers of women entering the workforce. Almost 60% of the women in the United States work outside the home. That's quite a contrast from 1964 when women comprised only 40% of the workforce. Today, women have higher expectations than ever before; as many as 25% of married women earn more than their spouses.

Men and women are also entering nontraditional jobs more frequently. Men are entering nursing and word processing fields, while women are becoming physicians and psychologists. Furthermore, society continues to evaluate people by what they do for a living and not necessarily for the quality of their relationships, the kindness of their children, or the balanced family life that they produce.

As mothers have reentered the workforce, so too have fathers taken a greater degree of responsibility in child raising as well as family life responsibilities. The buzz words for the families or parents of the new millennium are the "sandwich generation." Many modern parents not only have to care for their children, but are caring for their own parents who may have become too frail or disabled to care for themselves. Family may now include frail parents who need to live in the homes of their children.

So, the evaluation of family influence needs to take place with these considerations. The influence of the family on career decisions will be different from generation to generation depending upon the issues and demands that the family needs to contend with. These demands may prove to be exhausting and speak to the ubiquitous issue of work and life balance that affects the decision making of many college graduates in the new millennium.

Heather Nabozny

Let me start with an example of someone who demonstrates not only family influence, but important changes in workplace conditions as well.

Heather grew up in a family that owned a lawn care and gardening business. She developed her interests in lawn care by working with her father during her summer breaks. With this fledging interest in lawns and gardening, she went on to Michigan State University (known for its agricultural programs) to receive a degree that specialized in grass management. With her degree in hand, she decided to care for the most beautiful and prestigious lawns in the United States, those in professional baseball parks. Her first position was with the Toronto Blue Jays spring training facility. From there she headed off to Grand Rapids, Michigan, where she worked as a groundskeeper for the Michigan Whitecaps, a class A farm team for the Detroit Tigers. She must have done a whale of a job because from there she was invited to Tiger Stadium.

When she was notified that she was being considered for the grounds keeping job with the Tigers, Heather immediately called her parents for advice and counsel. She had been shown the joys and creativity in lawn growing. The advice she sought from her family was more than feedback on her work. She also wanted advice on how the family was able to create balance in their lives with their business. Heather Nabozny is the first woman to become a head groundskeeper in major league baseball. Her decision was made in a new context with a broad array of variables to seek advice about.

Gathering Information

We all have many stories about the influence that our parents and family members have on the career decision making process. But some of this will come into sharper focus in the counseling office when a counselor takes a detailed history. These histories become stories, like Heather's, and can include information about family influence as well as the family's approach to balancing career and leisure experiences.

There are a variety of methods that are used to gather information to assess the influence of the family in career decision making. These have been articulated in some depth elsewhere (Gysbers, Heppner, & Johnston, 2003). Creating, using, and sharing the assessment tools aids all counselors in establishing new approaches in career counseling.

Decision making doesn't take place in a vacuum, but must be conceptualized to include factors like community, social and economic status, culture and relationships, and gender expectations, all factors that can be subsumed when viewing the family of origin. When gathering information about the family, these factors must come into play. So to begin with, here are several approaches that reflect methods of gathering appropriate information about family contextual variables in career decision making.

Norman Amundson

Amundson (1998) has developed a direct approach for using family members in career counseling; he invites them into the clinical sessions to serve as observers. So, an adolescent might be invited to a session along with at least one of the parents. Parents are given license to offer their points of view on labor market conditions and the like. But, most importantly, they are asked to give their perspectives on their children's abilities, interests, and personal characteristics as they relate to the work world.

Amundson has also involved significant others in larger communities. He has described inviting family and community members to career counseling sessions within the First Nation communities in Canada (McCormick & Amundson, 1997). Unlike traditional career counseling sessions, these meetings have some innovative features like the utilization of talking sticks, eagle feathers, and ceremonial prayers. Individual clients are placed in the position of stating what their roles and responsibilities are, publicly, in front of their own community. The clients are able to receive support from the community while they make their commitments public.

Amundson believes that when significant others, family members or community members, are unavailable for in-person contact, information may be obtained by eliciting feedback on a questionnaire that he developed.

Exercise

The questionnaire is included and readers may wish to complete the instrument for themselves. Pick a family member who is in a career search or job change and fill in the material to share at a later time.

Amundson's Significant Other Questionnaire
(Amundson, 1998, p. 172)

Please complete the following questions. Your opinion is important to help make future career plans: Therefore, your honesty is greatly appreciated.

1. What would you say this person is good at? What skills has this person demonstrated?
2. What would you see as this person's major interest areas?
3. How would you describe the personal characteristics of this person?

4. What positive changes have you noticed over time in this person, especially in relation to work or looking for work?
5. In what ways could this person improve?
6. If you were to suggest the ideal job or career prospect for this person, what would it be?

Amundson suggests that the counselor work with the client to decide who would be among the best choices in the family to provide this information. The information can be debriefed with both the client and family member visiting the career counselor together.

Terry Taylor

Terry Taylor (2003), in her career counseling and consulting practice in the San Francisco Bay Area, has a worksheet that she asks her students and some of her clients to fill in. Her focus is generational, and she invites people to interview six individual family members or close family friends from at least three different generations about their work and careers. In the current generation, she suggests that siblings, spouses or partners or cousins be interviewed. She asks that information be obtained from the parents' generation, which could include parents, stepparents, foster parents, and, of course, aunts and uncles. Finally, she asks that information be obtained from representatives of the client's grandparents' generation and, whenever possible, the great-grandparents' generation. This can also take account of great and great-great aunts and uncles.

After making the selection of the six people, she asks that clients or students gather information about a host of work experiences of the interviewee including first jobs, favorite jobs, and relationships at work. To complete the exercise, Taylor suggests that the interviewee give four "tips" or important pieces of advice to the client.

With this approach, the family history that is gathered provides an opportunity for a client to explore some of the past that creates family myths and legends. The history also provides a template for further information gathering to discover what attributes a client has that may be generational.

Exercise

You may wish to complete Taylor's Family Work History using the following form. Remember that six individual family members from at least three generations are to be used. For each interview, ask and record the following:

Your first work experience—paid or unpaid
    Your age and approximate year of the experience
    Where did you work?
    What did you do?
    Was this full- or part-time?
    What was the pay scale?
What was your favorite job?
    Where did you work?
    What were the job responsibilities and duties?
    Was this full- or part-time work?
    What was the pay scale?

What was your favorite company or employer? What made this experience your favorite?

What is your current work status?
    Your age and approximate year of the experience
    Where did you work?
    What did you do?
    Was this full- or part-time?
    What was the pay scale?

For those who are retired, what was your last work experience?
    Your age and approximate year of the experience
    Where did you work?
    What did you do?
    Was this full- or part-time?
    What was the pay scale?

What are four tips or pieces of advice that you would offer to a family member regarding work and career development?

Understanding Vicarious Learning—Balancing Work and Life

Children today feel that they're programmed by the particular rhythms of their parents' schedules. Often they want to be listened to on their own schedule, not that of their parents. Children's attitudes about work may be a reflection of how they felt intruded upon by the work of their parents. If the job was always taking a parent away, so that the child was either left alone or latchkeyed, then maybe that child didn't develop a particularly positive attitude about work. In most family experiences, the best times may have been those that were spontaneous and unpredictable and had nothing to do with schedules.

Negative attitudes about work are sometimes brought home like unwanted leftovers. How many times do parents return home complaining about how tough the day was before they've closed the door? What do you think is communicated about the importance of work with this kind of an attitude? If parents complain about work excessively, what do you think the attitudes of their children toward work will be?

I've found it increasingly useful to gather some information on the role of work in the family of origin and the degree to which there was a balance of work and family life. Often the attitudes and decisions that we have about work are reflected in the way we watched family members go about their work. This has been referred to as vicarious learning and can have an important impact. John Krumboltz was influenced by being exposed to the work of his lawyer father. Other clients are similarly impacted.

It's curious to determine if the family put career or family first. Addictions like workaholic behavior can also be ascertained in the study of career and life balance. And pressures among the impoverished can be manifested by family members working two full-time jobs. NBC newscaster and political analyst Tim Russert (2004) wrote a book about his father holding two different jobs in Buffalo, New York, so that the family had income stability.

Brian

My client Brian felt lost in his career. Like Zac Unger from Chapter 1, he came from three generations of physicians. But what he remembers most vividly about the experience was that the men were always away and the opportunity for interaction was lacking. Fact is, Brian thought that his father was really kind of depressed being a physician and had a "tail wagging the dog" experience with it. He remembered cancelled or adjusted plans that resulted from his father not being able to take time off work.

The family was shocked when Brian decided that he would be a teacher. When they asked him about it, he said that he had three reasons for choosing that profession, "June, July and August."

So, with these thoughts in mind, I've found that it's useful to gather some information from clients on the manner in which the family was able to balance work and life, particularly in this era of two-worker families.

Exercise

I have developed the following brief questionnaire to assist in gathering information about the balance between work and life. You're invited to fill this in.

Chope's Career Life Balance Questionnaire

---

1. How many adult workers were there in your household?

2. Did they work full- or part-time?

3. What type of work did they do?

4. Did they seem to enjoy what they did?

5. Do you recall your parents juggling their schedules?

6. Did they ever seem to you to be out of control?

7. Besides yourself and siblings, did your parents have responsibilities for other family members?

8. Did they ever bring work home?

9. Did their work seem to interfere with your being able to spend time with them?

10. What times do you recall enjoying with them like meals, entertainment, vacations?

11. Did the activities of your daily life seem rushed or were the household schedules pretty well organized?

12. Did you experience or your parents experience any stress because of the work schedules of your family?

13. Did this occur on a regular basis?

14. Did the family need any special services like child care or elder care services?

15. Did the family need to use social or family services?

16. Did the family share responsibilities?

17. Were you able to participate in all of the extramural activities that you wanted?

18. Did you feel that your parents or other extended family members were available to you?

19. How well do you think that your parents balanced their work and family life?

20. How has this experience affected how you will balance your work and family life?

Family Constellation Questionnaire

Peterson and Gonzalez (2005) have created a family constellation questionnaire to assist with understanding family influence in terms of family and social context. This tool serves as a template to gather information on the following factors:

- Racial and ethnic background
- Major influences in your career decisions
- Mother's occupation, father's occupation
- Number of brothers and sisters
- Your place in the birth order
- Education of parents
- Career expectations of the parents for the children
- Parents' marital status
- Occupations of all four grandparents.
- How many times have you changed careers?
- Are you satisfied with your current career choice?

While some authors may have suggested the incorporation of family influence into the career counseling process, their impact has been limited because they didn't add any new counseling techniques in this area. But Amundson, Taylor, myself, and Peterson have developed protocols to make the information gathering and utilization process systematic. In addition, these protocols can be used in large group settings, unlike the career genogram which will be considered next.

The Genogram

Currently, the best known tool for information gathering about family influence in career decision making is the career genogram (Okiishi, 1987). It gives career counselors a well defined technique that can be easily used to explore the influence of the immediate and extended family. The genogram also allows for the exploration of current as well as historical, multigenerational career development patterns. The roles, behaviors, and attitudes of family members, along with the unfulfilled goals of specific family members, can be explored with this tool.

Family patterns of all types can be easily identified and aligned with the pressures of not measuring up to certain family standards. With a genogram in front of them, career counselors can develop new clinical perspectives and ask new questions.

The genogram is like a family tree that allows for the exploration of the genetic and cultural development of career identity while it isolates some of the more important root sources and influences. It really is a simple and marvelous tool. It allows for the origin of career expectations from the family. In this context, it can help define family judgments about career choices and definitions of success. It shows career choices over generations and the patterns of career choices over generations. It can be used to make career planning more imaginative, using family networks and connections as a base. It allows for people to separate out their personal life choices from those of their family.

There are many places where the family can be a principal in gathering biographical data about the client as a child and sharing that information. To that extent, the genogram can incorporate the entire family in a manner that is similar to completing Taylor's protocol. Parents as well as siblings, cousins, aunts, and uncles can play a role.

Families of origin and extended families can give a rich perspective to a client's particular strengths and weaknesses. In making a career choice, bouncing ideas off different family members sharing a common ancestry gives an uncanny, genetic view of what people in the shadows of the client have experienced. The National Career Development Association now recommends a greater use of family stories to talk about the unfolding of career choices.

However, preparation of the genogram for many modern families may be a daunting task. The traditional family, with delineated roles of provider and nurturer, is difficult to find and the genogram can become artistically "messy" with a complicated family structure.

Creating a Career Genogram

The best method of creating a genogram is to gather historical information. It is often worthwhile to create a chart like the one below and then have relatives and friends of the family fill in some of the pieces. While some people think that it is useful to include birth dates, I believe that these are often difficult to extract and tend to discourage people from creating the genogram. I think it is best to isolate the relatives and then determine their educational backgrounds and work experiences, focusing primarily upon what they might call their career. You can begin by listing the work of your four grandparents. Some people who really get into this decide to go back even further, but for convenience sake, I believe that going back to the grandparents is quite enough. Then you should add their children. That would include your parents, aunts and uncles. Then you can add yourself and your siblings and cousins.

Mother's side   Grandparents   Father's side

_____

_____

Aunts and Uncles

_____

_____

Cousins

_____

_____

Parents and/or stepparents

_____

_____

Brothers, sisters, and yourself

_____

_____

_____

With this information in hand, you can go ahead and construct your own genogram that looks like the one included here. The genogram is an unstandardized procedure, so there are many different ways of constructing one. Currently, there are over 8,000 general genogram web sites on the Internet, so many examples are available. The words "career genogram" will elicit close to 800 Web sites. There are also many symbols indicating events like divorce, death, and illnesses that can be used in the genogram for historical purposes, should you wish to have an increase in the complexity. You can simply type in the word "genogram" into your browser and begin. I believe that you can accomplish this easily by focusing upon only the educational levels and the career choices of each of the people on the genogram. You can also log onto www.genogram.org or www.genopro.com for additional guidance.

Betty's Genogram

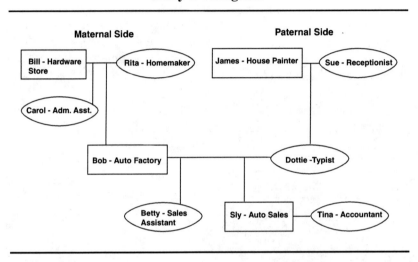

Betty was a sales assistant to a sales manager for ten years. She was unmarried and wanted to explore why she stayed in her job for so many years and why she was uninterested in a relationship. The genogram that she prepared showed that career stability was a trait that had been handed down for generations. Her grandfather had always said that having a roof over your head and food on the table were the two ingredients that made life hassle free. Betty had taken his words and those same reinforcing remarks of her father and mother to heart. Career fulfillment was less important in her family than career stability. But Betty wanted more. She hoped to begin to take classes in the local community college and she wanted to branch into areas that she had only dreamed of. She wanted to pursue an Associate Arts degree in English with the hope that she could go on to a four year college. Of course, there was family resistance to the idea. But through viewing the genogram, Betty realized that no one in the family had ever branched out to utilize higher education. She saw the family as ordinary, and she wanted to feel more special.

The genogram is the starting point in assessing family influence. Follow-up questions can aid understanding and illuminate different patterns between generations. When you finish the genogram, you might continue with a series of questions. You ask these of yourself or a client you may be working with. They are drawn from *Dancing Naked* (Chope, 2000).

> What family patterns exist?
> Which family members had a clearly formed work identity?
> Which family member did you most admire?
> Who did you identify with?
> Whose career aspirations are most similar to your own?
> Which person was most influential in the creation of your own career identity?
> What pressures do you feel when you compare yourself to your family?

You might also want to consider an additional series of questions that John Dagley (1984) has found useful:

> What were the dominant values in the family?
> What ghosts or legends existed?
> Are there any family myths that transcended generations?
> What about family secrets?
> Are there any pressures that emanate from "unfinished business" in the family?
> What family interaction rules have been passed along?
> Who was vocal and who was silent?
> How did the family balance learning, working, and playing and how were these valued?

As you can see, the genogram can elicit a substantial amount of information. The genogram can also be used to help couples interpret significant differences in their perceptions of careers. Career issues can be an ongoing source of strife in relationships, and so the genogram can be used as a therapeutic tool to help couples sort out material.

The genogram will generally elicit memories of what your relatives said about you when you were little. Thoughts like, "Gee, you really are going somewhere" or "Your dad expects you to go to Princeton" are forever running through the perceptive mass of many adults. These are made more evident by exploring with the genogram.

Even with the protocols and genograms, there are many more questions that could be asked. In addition, the protocols mentioned do not organize family influence data in a systematic way that can easily be used by a clinician. With this in mind, I created a new protocol.

A New Protocol

Using examples from my own professional experience and drawing from new research on the qualitative study of relational influences (Schultheiss, Kress, Manzi, & Glasscock, 2001), I have developed the following new protocol for counselors to use in gathering information about the impact of the family on career decision making. Through helpful comments and feedback from colleagues, I created the protocol consisting of six primary questions. This is a form that has been presented elsewhere and continues to be a work in progress (Chope, 2001a, 2002, 2003).

The protocol may be used to elicit important information from a client's history. It offers a unique strategy for gathering, organizing, and understanding data on the influence of the family in career decision making. But the protocol goes beyond simply gathering information. That's what makes it so useful to clients and clinicians alike.

It consists of the following questions that you may ask your clients. You may also fill in the information for yourself. I have included follow-up questions that can be asked within each primary question.

The protocol at first appears to have a middle class slant to it. But it has proven to be a useful tool in many workshops with a multiethnic, multicultural, and diversified clientele. What makes the protocol most helpful is the systematic logic and the series of follow-up questions which help guide and deepen the exploration of family influences.

1. What kind of career related information did the family provide?
2. What tangible assistance was provided and were there strings attached?
3. What type of emotional support did the family provide?
4. Was the client concerned about the impact of the career choice on the family?
5. What disruptive family events affected the client or other members of the family?
6. What were the actions of family members who were asked to help and actions of those who were not asked to help?

Exercise

Each question invites a different type of exploration as the following will illustrate. You are invited to fill in whatever information you can.

QUESTION 1. What kind of career related information did the family provide?

Several follow-up questions can provide useful information.

A. Did the family help the client generate different possibilities and new experiences?
B. What alternatives did the family suggest regarding schools, training or careers? How did these affect the client?
C. What was the family's impression of gender roles? How did these affect the client's career choices?
D. What family traditions or legends existed?
E. Was there any "forced guidance," a tendency to push the client in a direction more reflective of the family's interests than those of the client's?

Sometimes a person's career can evolve because the family is in a particular business and has a sense of what is necessary to create in order to be successful. For example, the comedian Albert Brooks, one of the purportedly funniest people in America, was born with the name Albert Lawrence Einstein. His father was a radio comedian and his mother was an actress and singer. His friends in high school were Richard Dreyfuss and Rob Reiner. The rest of his family was also affected by the careers of the parents. His brother became a comedy producer, and another brother is an advertising executive, while his half-brother is a baseball writer.

The projected fantasies of a family often far outweigh the information base and realities of the job market. It's always interesting for college and high school counselors and advisors to watch family members at a secondary school college information and advising night. Frequently, the family will try to steer their offspring toward those people, schools, or programs that they feel are the best for their child. Career counselors should determine whether there was any "forced guidance," opinions given without the consideration of the client.

Counselors should also be aware of the family's impressions of particular roles that men and women played in the workforce. Men who choose to be paralegals or nurses frequently embarrass some traditional parents because they perceive these roles as distinctively feminine.

Finally, what career information came from family tradition? Did the family ensure that only particular schools or career paths would be followed because that reflected positively upon the status of the family? I've had many clients who came from small- and medium-sized family businesses who did not want to pursue these endeavors. Yet the family hammered them with evidence that involvement in the business would be economically prudent as well as beneficial for the family.

QUESTION 2. What tangible assistance was provided and were there any strings attached?

    A. Were tuition, books, and supplies provided?
    B. Was transportation provided to attend school or get to a job?
    C. Was housing provided or made available?
    D. Were incidentals taken care of?
    E. Was health insurance paid for until the age of 23?

Clients tell me regularly that their parents made an unsolicited offer to pay for graduate school as long as the client went to the graduate school or program of their parents' choice. The counselor should be aware of the emphasis the family placed upon the role of money in life and culture and whether money was used to "blackmail" a client.

QUESTION 3. What type of emotional support did the family provide?

The counselor can also follow up with another question. Who was supportive and who was not? And the following questions can elicit deeper understanding.

    A. How certain was the client that emotional support would be available, no matter what?
    B. Did the family take a hands-off but supportive approach?
    C. Was there subtle emotional pressure to pursue a particular path?
    D. Was the client told by the family to "just be happy?"
    E. Was the client told that his/her plans wouldn't amount to much?

What the counselor should know is how certain the client was that emotional support would be given, no matter what the client chose to do. That kind of support is truly priceless and allows for an appreciation of trusting the intuition of the child. This type of support lends itself to a client being able to apply one of the Gelatts' paradoxical principles of being focused and flexible about what you want (Gelatt & Gelatt, 2003). Knowing that emotional support will be available allows for a career decision maker to balance the achievement of established goals with discovering new and different goals.

It's important to know if the family took a "hands off," but supportive approach to the client's decision making. Sometimes clients report, "My parents just wanted me to be happy." But was that emotional support or pressure? Many of my own clients have felt that it was somewhat of a burden to be told that they should be happy.

It's conceivable that the family chose not to be involved because they were uninterested in the career pursuits of their children or had preconceived limitations of what any of their children would amount to. Behavior such as this could have resulted in the client becoming indifferent to career choices. I have found that those career seekers who were not given much support and were told that they should have lowered career expectations became somewhat indecisive in choosing a career path. This type of historical information should be uncovered by the counselor.

It's also important to find out whether the family attempted to dissuade the client from a particular plan. Families can be quite self serving. For example, a business owner who wants a child to enter business school and support the family business may resent the fact that the child wishes to pursue a career like film making which is at odds with the wishes of the family.

Saleem

Saleem, a South-Asian client of mine, had to make the rugged choice of not obeying her parents. She married a man her parents wanted her to marry, but with whom she was never in love. After her divorce, she returned to college to pursue a degree in art. Her parents wanted her to major in accounting. She felt little emotional support from her family for her career and life decisions. But, on the other hand, her parents, who remained in India wanted her to be happy, stay in contact, and provide housing for her sisters who might move to the United States to continue their educational programs. Eventually, she received her degree in art, but she felt wrongly judged by the family for her divorce and her lack of interest in accounting. Her self-esteem was affected by her enrolling and failing first year accounting twice. She felt no emotional support from the family, and this hindered her confidence as she tried to obtain work in advertising and commercial art.

Saleem's issues show a blending of career-related, multicultural, and emotional issues that are very difficult to resolve. Knowing the lack of support from the family allowed the counseling work to become more intensified and focused on the intersection of work and her relationships.

In more supportive circumstances, as pointed out by Amundson, the family perspective may be enormously helpful emotionally. These are the times when issues of culture and diversity can be explored in the context of positive perspectives on how a child might pursue particular work with passion. Moreover, in other circumstances, some family members who have suffered the humiliation of discrimination and prejudice may be called upon to give a perspective on how to confront these issues today.

QUESTION 4. Was the client concerned about the impact of the career choice on the family?

This question suggests that some focus of the career counseling sessions should explore attitudes that may have developed around the success of one sibling at the expense of another. Some siblings share rivalries about the amount of money that may have been spent on one sibling, but not the others. Clients of mine who have attended private boarding schools and colleges have suggested that their siblings were often jealous of this fact and, indeed, engaged in dark humor regarding their feelings. Differential costs and attitudes about perceived unfairness can affect how different family members become motivated to achieve.

Janet

My client Janet told me that she always felt guilty that she had gone to a private preparatory school for girls in Providence, Rhode Island, and then went on to Smith College. Her parents had spent a veritable fortune on her education, so she said; and she felt that her two brothers were always angry about it. One brother completed high school and was a contractor like her father, and her other brother finished a state college for teachers and was a certified teacher in Boston. Janet was a director of human resources for a high technology firm in Santa Clara, California. Her success was marred by the guilt she had experienced around the different educational and career opportunities afforded to her. While the brothers were proud of her accomplishments, they continued to tease her about being the favorite child or the bright light in the family. She felt that the experience affected her brothers' career paths.

Some clients want to seek input from their families in order to consider the ramifications that their choice will have for all of the other members of the family. It's difficult to put this kind of burden upon someone who wants to be rewarded for having good grades in school and being motivated to achieve. However, there are consequences. Although this initially promotes harmony in the family, it can also lead to negative self talk years later that had the client not always looked out for the family, he or she may have had a more satisfying career path.

Two years ago, I worked with a surgical resident who said that his parents always wanted him to be a doctor and would have been heartbroken if he had chosen another path. But his younger brother and sister resented his receiving so much attention and family resources. The brother and sister felt cheated that they had to do without so that their older brother could finish medical school. The irony is that after the death of his parents, my client was considering leaving the practice of medicine.

The case shows how clients with siblings may choose to discuss issues of fairness and birth order. The surgical resident perceived the family very differently than his siblings. He felt it was unfair that he had so few choices; his siblings felt he took all the attention. In contrast to the above, a first child who attended college when the family had fewer resources may feel put out when compared to younger siblings who weren't asked to contribute as much to their educational and career related costs.

It's important to keep in mind that a successful sibling might prove to be emotionally demanding for the other members of the family. And the other siblings can bring shame upon the family when their career paths didn't turn out as the family had expected. President Jimmy Carter's brother Billy embarrassed him and the White House from time to time (Public Broadcating Service [PBS], (n.d.)). Baseball Hall of Famer Dennis Eckersley was born two years after his brother Wally. While both Eckersley brothers were good athletes and, as it turns out, alcoholics, Wally is in prison with a 40-year sentence while Dennis is considered one of the greatest closing pitchers in baseball history. In 2004, he was inducted into the Baseball Hall of Fame (Bodely, 2004).

QUESTION 5. What disruptive family events affected the client or other members of the family?

Clients should explore any disruptions, such as geographical moves, unemployment, changes in marital and economic status, catastrophic regional disasters and the like, that affected the career development of their parents. Counselors should determine how these childhood disruptions may have affected the career development of their clients. Disruptions can also influence what clients remember about their childhood learning. I've counseled many children of military personnel who were uprooted themselves a number of times during their childhood and regret that they never seemed to develop strong friendships. This later affected their capacity to network well.

The Iraq War of 2003 and beyond will bear witness to the heavy impact that can be had among people who have had to take a year or more out of their lives to go to war as a reservist, when their expectation was that they would be spending two weeks a year as a "weekend warrior" with another weekend a month as a reserve soldier. In addition, for those people who have parents in full-time military activity, there will be uprooting that can affect educational and career choices.

In other cases, a calamity like the loss of a business can be devastating. In *Dancing Naked* (Chope, 2000), I wrote about my great-great grandfather, Edward Chope, who owned the largest carriage company in Detroit, the E. Chope & Sons Carriage Company. It was, indeed, an extraordinarily successful enterprise that the family was proud of. It happened that the automaker Henry Ford approached my grandfather with the idea that he could put one of the new gasoline powered engines he was working on into one of my great, great grandfather's carriages. Henry Ford thought that this was a remarkable opportunity for them both. But Grandpa Ed turned him down. He thought that Ford's idea wouldn't work; the automobile would need roads which weren't available and sources of fuel which didn't exist much beyond the borders of the city. Obviously, Ed was less than futuristic. But the consequences to him and to his work were devastating. Henry Ford went on to other carriage makers and, in five short years, our family was out of the carriage business.

Some clients are terrified of making a bad decision. They may especially fear making a mistake in a work world that's marked with so much turmoil. Accordingly, they may usher in the family to develop another perspective on their career path, to serve as a safety net. Many believe, often wrongly, that with the family's perspective they could make better predictions. Clients may seek familial advice because they're afraid of bringing shame upon the family for a career choice that's inconsistent with the family's culture.

Using the family in this way may be a reflection of the client's own self doubt. Clients are often afraid of pursuing their own uniqueness and thus will take a safer path generated by the family. They also have some tendency to compare themselves to others and need the family to help them to believe that they will measure up in a competitive job world.

Exercise

One of the exercises useful at this juncture is to have clients explore the critical incidents that have taken place that could be considered disruptive to their career path. It could be excessive moves, the death of a parent or close relative, separation or divorce, losing a job, the closing of a business, shame from a relative, felonious wrongdoing by a family member, or something as simple as moving away from home.

The exercise is simple. Draw a horizontal line and break it up into five year increments. The line should stretch from birth until the present time. In each five year interval, have the client write down at least five critical events that may have had an impact on his or her career decision making. These events can be personal or they can be related to the events that were taking place within that time period that appeared to be important. If the client didn't have any personal critical incidents, he or she should write down incidents from current events that may have affected how he or she viewed career possibilities. For example, in the last few years, we have had the Iraq War, the Enron and Imclone scandals, the bursting of the dot com bubble, and budget crises in a number of states. All of these exemplify events that can influence how people decide upon their career choices. These can also be personal issues like a struggle to fit in, getting laid off or fired from a job, and emotional responses to life changes, anything that could affect career choices.

After completing the critical incidents, you can have the client review what needs to be done to overcome some of the issues that may have a background in these events. Uncertainty about the future, self esteem issues, or simple choices about interests and career pursuits can be done with this in mind.

If your client is lost about how to do this, it is possible to do some family research by talking to other family members about family history, and it is possible to gather archival information from the Internet using one of the popular search engines or from local newspapers. Memories can also be elicited in the office by having clients recall influential people at different times in their lives.

There are many well known people who have had their lives disrupted by unfortunate events, but this has also impacted their careers in ways that could be deemed positive. Toronto-born Jim Carrey had an uneven childhood. He is the son of an accountant and stay-at-home mom who watched his father lose his job. The family became disoriented and homeless, and Carrey was miserable. He left school in the 10th grade so that he could find menial jobs to help the family out. Turns out, he was able to make a better income by doing impressions of people in comedy clubs. Watching his father lose a safe job inculcated in him a scary type of edginess to his work. But he was willing to take the risks of an actor because he didn't think that work would be stable anyway. He just wanted to be successful so that he could make his parents proud of him while he helped them out (Australian Broadcasting System [ABC], June 16, 2003).

QUESTION 6. What were the actions of family members who were asked to help and actions of those who were not asked to help?

This question is often one of the most difficult for clients, usually because they will need some time to think about it. But, after some speculation and homework, they can also come back to another follow up question which can go something like this. Of those who were involved, which were welcomed and which were not?

This question is framed using two categories from Phillips et al., (2001): actions of people who want to be involved in the client's process, even if they are not asked, and recruitment of people the client wants to ask to help.

Family members do become involved in the career development process of others even when they're not asked, and career counselors ought to probe about the kind of unsolicited involvement the family offered. These data allow for determining where pressure was placed on the client about family rules of order and tradition.

There is also a further question. Of those who were asked to help, who offered assistance and who did not?

Career counselors need to be sensitive to the manner in which the family responded when the client asked for assistance and to determine the level of support. Certainly, the family may respond for self serving reasons. Counselors can also use this information to determine how independent the client's decision making is. Some clients have a history of never making any decision independently. Others use consultation sparingly. But clients usually have good reasons to recruit other family members for advice, and the counselor should know these reasons.

Probably the most telling example of problems in the family around career decision making occurs when a client is redirected away from his or her first or second choices of a career. David, the unhappy urologist from Chapter 1, is a perfect example of what can go wrong when someone is dissuaded from following his or her passions.

So What Can Be Achieved with This Assessment Process?

There are a variety of places where family assessment information can be useful. Here are four to remember:

First and foremost, family interaction patterns can be understood and the family can learn to listen more and judge less. Family members can help by understanding their own meaning of success and how that meaning influences the rest of the family. The family may wish to rethink traditional measures of success. They can be assisted in changing their point of view and begin to help the client to define success with respect to what matters most to the client as long as the client acts responsibly.

With the discovery of history and values, family members and the career decision makers can begin to tailor an honest assessment of where discrepancies lie. The family can engage in better self-evaluation, and a counselor supplying information or working as a mediator can help both clients and family members reach compromises when there are conflicts.

Second, family members can help with difficult career issues. They can make a more honest assessment of the worth of education and training. They may be more sensitive to the wishes of their children, especially regarding the entering of a family business. They can also help with counseling about issues like whether a portfolio career might be more appropriate than a single full time job.

Learning about the stories and examples of other family members who have had these alternative choices can be very useful. Supportive family members can help to impart new information to clients, material that the client may be oblivious to.

Third, where appropriate, the family can learn to support risk taking and new ventures as the client explores alternative career paths. Knowing the past history and career stories of the family, there should be support for pursuing uncharted paths. The family might help the client to "think beyond the box" and serve as a creative "sounding board." The family can also be used as a resource to engage in further research. Family members can go online and research alternative occupations that may reflect their interests in their children and have more appeal to the child. Sample job titles, the typical career path, and the nature of the economics of the particular job can be easily researched. The family can also look for internships and on-the-job training opportunities when these appear to be appropriate. This approach could lead to an increase in the motivation of the career decision maker, even when some of the potential paths are at odds with the family. There is some evidence that families are more receptive to ideas when they are brought into the process. It seems that when parents are afforded some facts and are not kept entirely in the dark about the career prospects of their children, they are more amenable to some changes.

Fourth, assessment information can help to lead to good family discussions and beginning models of the networking process. This family networking process adds to the social integration of the client and can be a model for how he or she can do this with family members. A supportive family will teach the possibility of forging new connections and networks. Drawing from Roe (1957) and Bowlby (1982), those clients who have developed a sense of connectedness and partnerships through family networking are in a better position to develop stronger social connections and potential employment networks. The family, by example, assists with this and can work to maintain new and developing relationships to help other family members.

Chapter Summary

This chapter has presented an appetizer of qualitative questionnaires and protocols along with the career genogram which is now over twenty years old. Hopefully, you've had the opportunity to complete these and discover how they may be useful personally or clinically. As this field develops, there will be a need for more structured and quantitative tools for gathering information. What has been presented is just a beginning.

Chapter 5

The Nature of Decision Making

"Your vision will become clear when you can look into
your heart. Who looks outside, dreams;
who looks inside, awakes."
Carl Jung

There are a variety of ways that we make decisions. Intuition,
cultural mores, rational and nonrational thinking, and the Johari
window are among them. This chapter explores the decision
making process and gives you ideas about how different strategies
can be used that positively incorporate family influences.
Strategies will also be suggested for healthy methods of breaking
away from undesirable influences and constricting cultural
traditions.

In my tenure at San Francisco State University, I've advised many
students at both the undergraduate and graduate level about their career
plans. Our students hail from diverse populations, and over 200 cultures
are represented. But, regardless of academic discipline, the students,
without fail, talk about the effect of their families' influence on their career
and educational decision making process. In fact, family expectations
are regularly used by the students to help them to decide what they should
do with their lives. People who come from cultures steeped in tradition
often experience that influence and take to heart their family's preferences
in the decision making process.

In the San Francisco Bay Area, there's a heightened degree of
awareness of jobs in engineering and information technology, so many
students feel pressured to pursue education and careers in those lofty areas.
And, it seems that regardless of culture, there's the aged speculation that
the very best careers remain in the fields of medicine and law. Many
students feel bulldozed to enter these fields, even when there's not a lot of
evidence that they are either interested in the fields or will perform in
them successfully. Ironically, the unhappiest clients I counsel in my own
practice are successful lawyers in large, corporate law firms.

In general, while there will be many parents who feel fine about what their children are going to pursue, there are countless others who are upset when their children don't heed their advice. Oftentimes, parents feel protective toward their children, so they want the children to choose careers that will afford some degree of stability while allowing for a chance at independence.

Listening to the Parents

So why do college students and others spend so much time listening to their parents? There are a variety of reasons, but let's consider these. With their age and experience, parents have more career related information and exposure to the nuances of the work world. They also have a lifetime of historical and intuitive information about the children. Above all, they and perhaps their community have expectations for their children. Trouble is, the parents may not only be biased, their information may be faulty and their decision making outmoded.

But parents aren't the only determinants. By understanding different strategies, including those different from their parents, career decision makers can exercise independence with an upbeat, practical perspective, especially when they are at odds with their parents over the direction of their life path. Viewing problems and decisions from different angles, decision makers can become more hopeful about having the best possible methods of making decisions while addressing or avoiding parental conflicts. Using this approach, decision makers can even put some of the information that their parents and extended family provide to good purpose.

Exercise

Here's a short exercise to put family input into career decision making in context. Decide which members of your family had expectations for you in making your career choice. For those who did have expectations, go ahead and write down the strategies they used to convince you that they were right in their guidance. Then write down how their interventions affected you emotionally. That is, did they make you feel like you weren't going to succeed or that your decisions were a sign of your immaturity? Try to be aware of these internal feelings, even if they happened to be tortuous.

Expectations of Others

Families can have a negative impact on the way we make decisions.

Many negative cognitive decision making patterns of individuals arise because of expectations of family members. Parental expectations can be impossible to meet. Result? Often, there's self condemnation, guilt, anxiety, or depression. Clearly, family attitudes can affect an individual's self-esteem making him or her feel idiotic, limited, or weak. George Wein's story and his struggle for respect provide a good illustration.

George Wein

For more than half a century, George Wein has served as the founder and impresario of the world renowned Newport Jazz Festival. He's credited with creating an unparalleled respect for jazz, and his festival has served as a model for over 1000 new jazz festivals worldwide (Gans, 2004). George was the son of a physician who was quite upset about George's pursuit of a musical rather than a medical career. Turns out that George's piano playing was not what earned him fame, but rather his capacity to promote music. He's now the chief executive of Festival Productions which takes on more than 20 major events each year including the JVC Jazz Festival in New York and the New Orleans Jazz and Heritage Festival. His Festival Productions have helped to lead to the inclusion of jazz in college and university classes and a variety of cultural institutions.

So where does the family come in? George's father's message of respect became a theme for him. Although he didn't enter the health care field, George took on his own mission to earn the respect of his family and community. He's said that he wanted to see jazz accepted as an art form. He felt that if jazz were respected it would help him to earn the respect in his life that he desired.

The Risks Involved in Decision Making

All decisions involve risk. Career and educational decisions are among the diciest because these make people feel they can't turn back after a decision is made. Students reflect that even picking a college major feels so "final." The decisions are also difficult because of the ubiquitous expectations and evaluative expressions that different family members have, ones that can be impossible to meet. The result may be emotional self-flagellation. Students report that family attitudes and evaluations toward their decisions often adversely affect their self esteem. With this in mind, adopting strategies for decision making could offer ways to avoid some of these emotional pitfalls.

Strategies for Decision Making

There are two folk methods that are typically used by people making decisions. One is the use of intuition and the other is the use of cultural references. Of course, there are still a few who make their decisions by the flip of a coin, but that won't be given more space than a footnote.

Intuition

One of our most popular decision making methods is the use of intuition. The word intuition comes from the Latin "intuire," and refers to looking, regarding, or knowing answers from within yourself. Intuitive decision making doesn't proceed in careful, well-designed steps. Rather, it involves a more global perception of a problem. The uncalculated process by which intuitive types arrive at career decisions can be perplexing for career counselors.

Intuitive decision makers go with their gut, not necessarily basing behavior on any firm data or intricate cognitive processing. They figure that an idea or plan is going to unfold the way that they hope. When people use their intuition regularly, they tend to think about future possibilities, and they've had some success following their hunches in the past. They aren't necessarily rational with the process; they just have a nonbookish feel for whether or not some decision is going to work.

An intuitive hunch may be accompanied by a sense of compulsion, a feeling or a need to act immediately. That, too, is difficult for a career counselor to handle because the clients feel they need to heed these promptings.

Intuitive decision making can't be deconstructed into smaller elements, nor can it be easily explained. But there are some who claim that its value is unparalleled as a method for making difficult choices. People involved in life and death careers like police officers and firefighters are known to rely heavily on their intuition when making decisions. And corporate leaders interviewed in publications like *The Wall Street Journal* report that their superior decision making is related to their acute intuitive abilities.

Culture

The second nonsystematic way that people make decisions is based upon their culture and the rules of order that have been a part of their life since birth. Some of the material in this book is designed to help people address conflicts between what is demanded from their culture and what they feel they want. But, cultures have time honored methods and traditions that will drive the behavior of the members of the culture. Look at the impact of the Protestant work ethic on generation after generation of American workers.

Knowing that there are several ways to make decisions, even though they may not always seem or be rational, can be useful psychologically and tactically in confronting some of the beliefs and expectations of the family. There are strategies available to approach important decisions more systematically. We'll now turn our attention to four of these: the rational approach, planned happenstance, creative decision making through positive uncertainty, and self-efficacy.

The four methods of strategic decision making can enable decision makers to become conscious of how they might choose to proceed when selecting a career path. Being informed of these different methods can allow a person to employ a strategy that is different from one used by the family, especially if that isn't working.

Rational Decision Making

Let's take a look at the common rational way that people make decisions. This strategy involves a few steps—answers to questions—even though the actual making of a decision seems like an all or nothing prospect. The questions go like this:

1. What's the problem? Or, what's the decision that needs to be made?
2. What's the goal?
3. What's the probability of reaching the goal?
4. What are the alternatives to the goal?
5. What additional information is needed?
6. What choice should be made?
7. How can the choice be implemented?
8. How is the choice to be evaluated?

We will examine each of these steps in more depth.

What's the Problem? Or, What's the Decision That Needs to Be Made?

Good decision making is really good problem solving; and before you or anyone else can solve any problem, you need to be very clear about what the problem is. Asking simple questions can help. Try these as examples. What's not working now? What's stressful about my current situation? What do I need to change? Other questions, like what should my major be, or what career path should I choose, are too complex at this stage and need to be made simpler. When thinking about a major, you might want to ask which classes seem interesting. And, in looking to a career, you might want to consider the people whom you admire most and the career choices they made.

Obviously, all problems don't have equal weight nor is every solution equally difficult. When thinking about problems or decisions that need to be made, they can be characterized as major decisions, minor decisions and unpleasant decisions. A major decision might be what to major in. A minor decision could be what to wear to a party. An unpleasant decision might be to give up the idea of going to law school.

What's the Goal?

Sometimes there's confusion between the problem and the goal. A problem might be something on the order of "I don't know what to major in." The goal might be to become a successful person in a human resources department. So the goal needs to work in concert with the solving of a problem or making a decision. Decision making really involves the creation of a path and is almost never an experience that's all or nothing. My dissertation adviser at the University of Minnesota, David Campbell, used to tell his advisees, "If you don't know where you're going, you're probably going to end up somewhere else" (personal communication, 1972). He later wrote a book using this phrase.

Creating goals will necessitate change. And change is often unpleasant because it takes people into uncharted territory. People don't like to move into circumstances that are unpredictable. As a result, people often stay in the same jobs and relationships even when they aren't working because making changes can be so uncomfortable.

Fact is, though, in the world of career decision making, change is inevitable. Not many years ago career experts said, unequivocally, that people would experience four or five career transitions. Today that number is closer to nine or ten. Take Jeanie. She's only 34, has a biology degree from USC, and already has had four different careers: laboratory technician, information technologist, corporate communications writer, and public relations manager. Now she's considering returning to school in an executive MBA program. Her parents are frantic. She believes, rightly so, that her experience is more representative of the work world of the 21st century.

There isn't much in the way of career stability anymore, a fact that many parents don't accept. There are new and unfamiliar paradigms everywhere. Labor unions don't have the power they once had, and even college professors like me are fighting battles over the retention of time honored tenure policies.

Jeanie is not an unusual case. With the career marketplace changing so rapidly, institutional change is fast and opportunities pop up in any circumstance, leading to the possibility of innovative job choices and career paths. Problems will constantly crop up and some goals may need to be more fluid than people had anticipated.

Having goals should help to generate a few other questions. You might ask about what will be different or changed in your life when you meet a particular goal. Meeting some goals doesn't necessarily create internal satisfaction, and more than one of my own clients has wanted to turn back the clock and undo a change we had worked on. The most emotionally demanding part of the goal setting experience is deciding upon what you hope to accomplish with this goal.

What's the Probability of Reaching the Goal?

Speculating about goals is one thing; evaluating the probability of reaching them is something else entirely. It's important to honestly explore the possibility as well as the probability of reaching a goal. It's also necessary to isolate and examine any barriers to reaching a goal and to accept that some life goals may never be possible. I won't ever climb Mount Everest, swim the English Channel, or run the Ford Motor Company, all goals I had set for myself years ago.

Some goals may be possible, but not necessarily probable. As much as I would relish the experience, this book will probably not sell a million copies. Possible, yes. Probable, no. After looking at possibilities and probabilities, it's important to look at the barriers that keep you from reaching particular goals. These may be able to be overcome, increasing the probability of reaching a goal.

Barriers to Goals. Barriers to goals come in two forms, often summed up in the familiar saying, "Sticks and stones will break my bones, but names will never hurt me." External barriers are consequences of the environment and of the current reality we live in. These types of barriers can also be summed up in specific educational and experiential experiences that are lacking as well. I don't have the education or experience to run the Ford Motor Company, and I'm no longer in shape to climb Mount Everest. Educational level, health, appearance, and socioeconomic status have always been potential barriers to achieving goals.

There are also internal barriers, the infamous internal dialogue that you use that keep you from both enumerating and achieving your goals. Internal barriers are the well conditioned beliefs that you have about yourself that prevent you from acting just the way that you want to. I've listed many examples of these in *Dancing Naked* (Chope, 2000). They include:

"I'm helpless. Who would hire me?"
"I can't start at the bottom again."
"I can't keep up."
"I'll never get what I want."

The internal dialogue could be your own. But it can also be the voices of the family with their well crafted scripts that create internal barriers. Decision makers need to discriminate between their own voice and ones that don't belong to them.

What Are the Alternatives to the Goal?

A useful way of getting beyond some of the barriers to reaching a goal is to create alternative goals. Acceptance to Harvard may be the goal for someone applying to medical school, but going to Loma Linda Medical School still gets you a medical degree and a chance to sit for the licensing exams. So, for every goal, there should be alternatives. Sometimes these alternatives can be added on to a career choice and eventually could be goals themselves. Portfolio careers are often made up of several career choices that a job seeker has been able to put together to add variety to a career path along with some economic protections.

Exercise

Creating Alternatives. For every goal, it's a useful brainstorming technique to come up with ten alternative goals. Sure, this sounds like a compromise; but it should be thought of as a chance to add some creativity to your planning. If you can name a goal for yourself, try to then enumerate ten alternatives related to the goal that are suitable to you. Then, rate each of the alternatives with a number from one to five that reflects the feelings you have about each of them. A "one" could be "acceptable" and a "five" could be completely "unacceptable."

If you're having difficulty with the exercise, then try this. Come up with seven uses for a brick. Obviously, you can use bricks to build a dwelling. But what other uses are there? Time yourself and make the list in three minutes or less. This type of practice activity can help you to become more divergent and creative in your thinking. Then, go ahead and complete the original list of alternatives.

Billy Beane. Billy Beane, the general manager of the Oakland Athletics, wanted to be the very best player he could be in Major League Baseball. He was a terrific player early in his life and when he went on to the major leagues, he expected a lot from himself. As voraciously as he worked, and with his marvelous baseball name, he never achieved the playing status that he or others predicted. When he left his playing days, he stayed in baseball as an alternative to entering a different line of work, still believing he could be the best at something in his sport. He discovered he had an eye for talented players, and he understood how to develop new players by capitalizing on an organization's farm team system. With these two skills, he's been able to achieve the stature of arguably one of the best general managers in baseball, producing contenders year after year on a low budget. Billy Beane wanted to be the best he could be. But the job tasks that made him among the best were not his athletic skills as much as the alternatives he had created for himself.

What Additional Information Is Needed?

In order to make good decisions, information is needed. And information about your goal should be gathered along with information on the alternatives. Gathering information is a lot easier than it used to be. Not many years ago, my clients had to go to the San Francisco Business Library or a community college career center to research career possibilities. I suggested that they consult with people at the Small Business Administration and the Service Corps of Retired Executives (SCORE) as well. This process took a lot of time and commitment.

Today, the information gathering process is made easier with the use of the Internet and the various search engines that are available. Companies and their executive leadership can be researched with a mouse click. Salary information and job prospects, sorted by cities, counties, and states, can be retrieved and studied. Every college in the country has a Web site to dispense information about courses, majors, and expenses. Many encourage people to apply. So the information gathering process is painless and uncomplicated. Still, many people don't take advantage of data like these and instead tolerate the beliefs of the family members who negatively judge career ideas, goals, and decisions with inadequate or outdated information.

What Choice Should Be Made?

If you've generated a first choice and an adequate number of alternatives, then a lot of the career decision making work is going to be weighing different alternatives against the first choice. Mulling these over should only be done after retrieving the best information available. Some alternatives will need to be eliminated, and the remaining alternatives can be ranked against each other and contrasted to the primary goals. Those that are neither possible nor probable should be evaluated first and either eliminated or put into another list of choices for future consideration. Many of those choices can require substantial change and probably the acquisition of new education and skills along with additional experience. The process demands that you're well focused upon the outcome that you want. It also requires that you imagine the kind of passion that you'll have for the activities associated with your choice.

It's useful to elaborate on the alternatives. Try to imagine what reaching a particular goal will amount to in the long run. Take someone who wants to be a cardiovascular surgeon. There's college, medical school, internships, residency, surgical residency, cardiovascular residency, and then establishing a practice. You get the point. An eighteen-year-old making this plan doesn't realize that the setting up of a practice may not take place until the age of thirty-five. When you play out the choice to the end result, you may discover that you don't want it if it requires so much preparation. Maybe another choice which can be close to the desired outcome of the first choice will, in the end, be the better choice for you.

How Can the Choice Be Implemented?

Now here's the tough part of any decision making process, making the commitment. There is often resistance to finalizing the decision or implementing a strategy. This is the time for hand wringing for the people who feel that they have no choice, can't choose, or don't want to take the responsibility for choosing. And, of course, they don't want to make a mistake, upset the family, or feel as if they have taken too big a risk.

Here is where all of the information that has been gathered can be weighed along with the alternatives available. A person using this rational approach will examine the pros and cons of the goal and each of the alternatives to the goal, then try to make a decision. More resistance can set in. A lot of time, research, and energy were invested in this process, and maybe the decision maker doesn't want to give up the well-researched choices for one goal. That's too bad. Career decisions don't work quite like that unless you choose to have three part-time jobs or work in a job that pays the bills while you add on some other part-time gigs that you have more passion about.

At this point, even with all of the information available, some people still make decisions as though they were flipping a coin. That method doesn't do justice at this point to all of the hard work that has gone into the process. Rational decision making is just that, rational. It's not driven by luck or intuition. You make the best decision you can based upon the best answers to the seven steps just presented.

How Is The Choice to Be Evaluated?

That is going to be up to the person making the decision. Did the choice launch new possibilities? Did the choice leave the person with the feeling of buyer's remorse? There are endless conflicts that people continue to have after they have made their choice. They compare themselves to others and "wonder what might have happened" had they chosen another path.

Involving the Family

The process of making a decision can be done without any information from the family. So how does the family get involved? In each of the steps, there's uncertainty and anxiety, and in order for people to feel that they're on the right path, they want some validation from others. Who else are they most likely to pick? So they pick those whom they feel they can trust, have their best interests at heart, and have known them for a very long time. Those folks have information about them and perceptions about them that they don't have available. So, for better or worse, they pick family members.

To understand further why family members are consulted in the decision making process, we can look at an interesting technique for how people gather information. People have blind spots, and they need help from others to fill in some data before going on and making a decision. We can fill in some blind spots with the Johari window.

The Johari Window

The Johari Window was developed by Joseph Luft, an emeritus professor from San Francisco State University and Harry Ingham (Luft & Hingham, 1955). The model allowed for a certain degree of speculation about how people relate to each other and how they protect themselves from each other. It's a good example of the changes that occur in the perceptions of yourself and other family members as you develop. It also shows the communication changes that take place as you disclose more information to your family members while they also disclose their perceptions about you and your life choices. This simple but useful and popular model has four quadrants.

Johari Window

	Known to self	Not known to self
Known to others	1 *Open*	2 *Blind*
Not known to others	3 *Hidden*	4 *Unknown*

The first quadrant includes information that is generally known to you and to others. It's referred to as the open quadrant. This quadrant can include information about particular behaviors and motivation. And, as people become accustomed to each other, this quadrant can undergo a substantial expansion. For example, siblings and peers may have first quadrants that are quite packed with information in contrast to the others. Initially, according to the authors, what is known by both children and parents may be small. But, over time, this quadrant can increase in information. The authors suggest that the four quadrants be given different sizes as a representation of the quantity of data inside each.

In the second quadrant, the self is essentially blind. Other people, like parents, extended family members, and friends, can assess characteristics that people are unaware of. If you chew with your mouth open, have sleep apnea, snore, or interrupt people on a regular basis, other people are conscious of these activities and behaviors even when you're not.

The third quadrant is called the hidden quadrant because it is filled with material people know about themselves, but refrain from telling others. Experiences, political thoughts, and certainly ideas you have about your career that are in opposition to your family are contained in the hidden quadrant. It's filled with secrets.

The fourth quadrant is an area of unknown activity and behavior. Career thoughts, ideas, and behaviors that are lying dormant are examples of material that would be in this quadrant. As you age and become more informed about the world, new possibilities and opportunities emerge that both you and your parents had been unaware of, but were made available through development. Finding out that you were a good debater or had a penchant for numbers and accounting may not be skills that emerged until later in your adolescence. This rising consciousness of previously unknown material is often an exciting experience for both yourself and other family members.

As people age, the quadrants assume different sizes. And a change in one quadrant is going to affect the size of the other quadrants. Sometimes these are drawn pictorially to show the potentially vast differences in sizes between the quadrants, depending upon the type of information that people have about themselves and each other. In early childhood, your parents knew more about you, so quadrant two, the blind quadrant might be very large while quadrant three, the hidden quadrant, and quadrant one, the open quadrant, may be quite small. When you begin to think about what career to pursue, your family members may have knowledge about you and the work world that you believe could be constructive. Again, quadrant two looms large. In other words, in an area that you are blind to, they may have a great deal of appropriate information. And because of this, they can be quite influential.

As you develop, there is more that is known to yourself as well as to family members, so the first, or open, quadrant may become larger than the others. The larger the first quadrant, the more there is the opportunity for trust and good communication between yourself and your family members. If the first quadrant is smaller, it could reflect poor communication that is fraught with withholding.

Why Do We Seek Consultation?

We need others to help us with career decisions because they involve choice, risk, and commitment to an educational-vocational plan. At every step of the way in the career decision making process, you have to choose among possibilities. But choosing is difficult; you can notice that in restaurants as people ask for advice about what to select from a menu. So we look for support in our choosing process. Rarely do people make decisions entirely by themselves, nor should they. But the family may not always be the best resource. The appropriate added input can, under the right circumstances, make the process easier. Conflicting input can make the process difficult.

Career decisions entail a certain degree of risk so that the more information that you have about yourself from others, the more you can alleviate some of the stress that you may feel from lacking essential information about the work world. We all look for some degree of control over our career and life plans, and increasing information will reduce some uncertainties. All decisions involve some degree of risk; and educational and career decisions are among the most risky, so the advice of others is frequently sought out. That keeps us from jumping into situations that may be expensive and time consuming and forces us to more expeditiously weigh our different choices. By using a tool like the Johari window, you may be able to prevent becoming your own worst enemy.

Further, career decisions also involve change and commitment. Since change and commitment also elicit stress, people tend to gravitate to their family members in order to alleviate their stress levels. If you really don't care about your career or educational choices, then you might let fate determine a decision. On the other hand, if you feel that you really want to engage in a particular career path, then there is more stress.

Basic Rational Career Decision Making Theory

Having described the strategic thinking in rational decision making, we can now demonstrate how several well known basic career decision theories fit into the rational decision making style. Trait and Factor Theory, Holland's theory, and the Theory of Work Adjustment will be briefly described as illustrations of rational career decision making that many people use with or without counseling.

Frank Parsons and Trait and Factor Theory

Almost 100 years ago, Frank Parsons, the identified founder of career counseling, suggested that for people to select a career they should have the following (1909):

1. A clear understanding of yourself, your attitudes, abilities, interests, ambitions, resource limitations and their causes;
2. Knowledge of the requirements and conditions of success, advantages and disadvantages, compensation, opportunities, and prospects in different lines of work;
3. True reasoning on the relations of these two groups of facts. (p.5)

Parsons' work is the foundation of the Trait and Factor Theory of career development, and the work influenced the development of the many career tests available. Tests of interests, values, aptitudes, and personality help people gather information about themselves. To use this theory to make decisions, you need to gather information about yourself.

Psychometric information from testing and personal history information can be gathered to enable self understanding. The Internet can be used to gather information about work requirements, compensation, opportunities, and availability. Web sites as repositories of information can be located easily with a search engine like Yahoo or Google. Then you can assess how your personal attributes fit the characteristics needed to enter the jobs or careers you are interested in. If you can't easily do this alone, then a counselor, advisor, mentor or coach can help relate the two together.

John Holland and RIASEC

John Holland (1985) views rational career choice differently from Parsons. While his theory is still a rational, trait and factor theory, its focus is more on work personality. Holland believes that career choices are an extension of our personalities; in a sense, a projected fantasy of who we think that we are. The career choices that people make are expressions of traits like their interests, values, and personal characteristics. People gravitate to different work environments because of these traits. Holland posits that there are six types of people (Realistic, Investigative, Artistic, Social, Enterprising, and Conventional) who are attracted to environments of the same name. No person or environment is a pure type, but is, rather a combination of two or three of these types. Career decisions are made by gathering information about your type through tests like the *Self Directed Search (SDS)* or *Vocational Preference Inventory (VPI)* and matching the type to different work environments that are available in Holland's book, *Dictionary of Holland Occupational Codes* (Gottfredson & Holland, 1989). A counselor can help clients to understand what type or types they may be and determine which work environments appear to be most suitable for them.

Dawis and Lofquist's Theory of Work Adjustment

The last rational approach to decision making described here is by Dawis and Lofquist (1984). They suggest that people make decisions based upon the degree to which they believe they will be satisfied on the job and will perform to a satisfactory standard. They, like others, have developed several inventories to gather information about worker skills and occupational needs. Then they match the worker's skills with the ability requirements of a job to gain a measure of job "satisfactoriness," or the degree to which a person can be expected to perform adequately on the job. They also measure occupational needs and match these to jobs which have the specific reinforcers to meet these differential needs. When a person's needs can be reinforced on the job, we say that the person can be satisfied by their work environment. Career decisions are made when people feel that they can be satisfied and function in a satisfactory way on the job. Job satisfaction and job satisfactoriness can result in greater job stability and the accrual of job tenure, provided that the job doesn't change dramatically or unexpected events like the selling of the company take place.

Exercise

Putting the theories into practice. Two instruments are available without cost that will allow you to use Holland's theory and the *Theory of Work Adjustment*. You can go to the O*Net Web site at www.onetcenter.org and follow the instructions for the *O*Net Interest Profiler* and the *O*Net Work Importance Locator*. The *Interest Profiler* will give you scores on the Holland RIASEC scales while the *Work Importance Locator* will give you information on your career needs based upon the *Theory of Work Adjustment*. Compare your interests and your needs to the occupations that are made available to you. Then look to see if your current educational and career plans are consistent with the information you've obtained. When you have completed the activity, you will have psychometric information obtained in a rational and positivistic way.

Non-Rational Career Decision Making Methods

There are also decision making methods that are categorized as non-rational. These are planned happenstance and positive uncertainty and are described below.

Planned Happenstance

A few years ago, City College of San Francisco Professor Kathleen Mitchell coined a new term about decision making titled "planned happenstance." The details of this are spelled out in an article that she prepared with John Krumboltz and Al Levin (Mitchell, Levin & Krumboltz, 1999). This creative and upbeat approach to decision making might be conceptualized as "making lemonade out of lemons." But essentially it asks how you can look for and make meaning out of the twists and turns of life. John Krumboltz and Al Levin have written *Luck is No Accident* (2004) which expands on a decision making model that has, as its focus, the process of constructing career opportunities when unexpected and unplanned events take place.

This approach is quite different from the rational approach and positivistic career decision making models just presented. And, it's a departure from Krumboltz's earlier social cognitive learning theory of career decision making. Rather than combining personal attributes and integrating them with the work environment, people might consider staying open to possibilities and creating new, unexpected prospects for themselves using creativity rather than practicality. Most family members will probably not be immediately accepting of this approach, and it certainly won't work for everyone. But it did work for Rick Peterson after his promising career as a major league pitcher was derailed by injury.

Rick Peterson. Rick Peterson is a pitching coach in major league baseball. He was the coach for the Oakland A's when they were managed by Art Howe; and a year after Howe left the A's to become manager of the New York Mets, Peterson moved over to assist him. Peterson has been described as a starving artist, physical education teacher, and baseball pitching coach (Jenkins, 2004). His father, Harding Peterson, had played for the Pittsburgh Pirates and later became their general manager. He later put together the 1979 World Series winning team easily identified with the song, "We Are Family."

So baseball was in Rick Peterson's genetic makeup. But his family wanted him to be a lawyer or doctor because these professions promised more stability than baseball ever could. But two events changed his life. The first was blowing out his arm through overuse as a pitcher for the Gulf Coast Community College in Panama City, Florida. Injury prevented him from achieving the pitching greatness that his baseball heritage predicted. But, while attempting to rehabilitate his pitching arm, he met a chiropractor who improved his arm and who also helped him to realize that in his heart he wanted to be a teacher.

Peterson was able to spend time at the American Sports Medicine Institute in Birmingham, Alabama, where he joined the staff to understand the nature of the pitching motion and how he could become an expert in preventing pitching injuries. He fashioned his craft. But baseball changes come about slowly. In spite of Peterson's knowledge base, he was often considered too advanced to be a coach and he had unusual techniques that people questioned. For example, he had his pitchers throw practice pitches to home plate with their eyes closed. (Interestingly, basketball legend Michael Jordan practiced throwing free throws with his eyes closed).

Nevertheless, with persistence Peterson has evolved into one of the most revolutionary pitching coaches of his time. He probably has the knowledge of an orthopedic surgeon when it comes to understanding the pitching motion. Yet he never went to medical school.

What we learn from Peterson is that there are a number of benefits to remaining open minded and trying new activities. Being able to develop passion for something that combined a variety of attributes, Peterson reinvented himself after his baseball injury. He focused upon his interest in teaching, coupled with his love of baseball and carved out a career that is filled with eagerness and enthusiasm.

The Happenstance Point of View. Approaching career decision making from a happenstance point of view takes issue with some of the common ideas that are suggested by folk wisdom and rational decision making. Here are a few examples of rational thoughts:

> Don't leave a job unless you've already got another one.
> Don't let unexpected events derail your educational and career plans.
> Know your dream and create a path to reaching it.
> Failure can cost you your job and ruin your shot at your dream.
> Hang onto your goals.

Rational choice perspectives and their varying pieces of advice have worked well before and they'll continue to work. But they don't work for everyone. What if you couldn't stand your job and wanted to leave today? If you are fired or redeployed, are you really in ruins? What if you, like Peterson, can never achieve your goals because of a disability? So, some career decision makers will need to forge new approaches to career decision making by actually creating lucky situations or realizing them when they exist and taking advantage of them.

Using this approach requires that people be more tuned in to their own needs as well as the potential needs of society. They need to become more observant. And they need to try new activities. I've been a sailor all my life, and I'm sorry I never learned to drive a tug boat. But if I had said to my parents at 18, "Get me a ride on a tug or a lake freighter or an ocean liner," maybe I would have been intrigued enough to consider an education at a merchant marine academy rather than a college. I think of this every time I am out on San Francisco Bay observing the tugs maneuver the ocean liner traffic through the shoals and estuaries.

According to happenstance theory, people are advised to keep their options open. If people aren't ready to commit to a career choice, they should be able to take a moratorium on the process and gather more experience and information rather than choosing something before they are ready. They'll need to give up on poor choices that haven't panned out. They need to be flexible and excited rather than scared about alternatives. And maybe they should give up on some dreams that they don't really embody as their own.

Essentially, the thinking behind happenstance decision making is that people should be willing to try new adventures. Jerry Brown was Governor of California and ran for president of the United States. At age 60, he became mayor of Oakland. He won a second term as well. Colonel Sanders was in his sixties when he founded Kentucky Fried Chicken.

In addition to trying new adventures, people should realize that mistakes can lead to new information. When Thomas Alva Edison regularly "failed" at finding the appropriate filament for his light bulb, people criticized him for his many mistakes. He said he didn't really make any mistakes, he now actually knew 276 materials that wouldn't work.

Another part of happenstance thinking is that people can generate their own luck by making things happen. People need to be active and network frequently to meet new people with new ideas. When an unlikely opportunity comes along, people should take advantage of it. If they need some help in deciding what to do, they can have a mentor help. With any new activity, they can begin with an action plan and take small, successful steps. And, if they can hold onto any mantra about career paths, it should be, "begin again." Creating luck demands the following according to Krumboltz and Levin:

> Adjust to or overcome barriers.
> Network with all types of people.
> Keep learning.
> Try new activities.
> Get involved in new projects.
> Take advantage of a new opportunity or idea.

Happenstance strategizing may be particularly useful when taking a new job and trying to adjust in a manner that could have been different from what has gone before. Clearly this is nonrational thinking and will be difficult to have a family steeped in tradition to accept. But planned happenstance would be a good approach for doubting family members to consider when confronted by a career seeker who wants to do something different from what the family had planned for.

An approach that has some similarity to planned happenstance and is another nonrational method of decision making is familiar to many career counselors and is called "positive uncertainty."

Positive Uncertainty

In 1989, H. B. Gelatt prepared a marvelous paper about decision making that launched a whole new decision making strategy, challenging many of the notions of the rational approach to decision making. He called the approach "positive uncertainty," a name which has been associated with him, and now his wife (Gelatt & Gelatt, 2003). They point out that when the future is certain, all you can do is prepare for it. But when the future is uncertain, as all of our career futures seem to be, then you should be part of actually creating a future rather than simply preparing for it.

The Gelatts focus on the future in decision making and they describe three kinds of future: the possible, the probable, and the preferable. They say that most rational decision makers will focus upon the probable and preferable futures, but rarely attend to the possible futures. What positive uncertainty promulgates is the creation of new possibilities.

They see rational decision making as limiting possibilities. Goals and preferences, they say, are rarely completed and are continuously changing, as you might have determined yourself by completing the exercises earlier in the chapter. With the work world changing, it's often difficult to maintain goals for an extended period of time. Furthermore, they suggest that decision makers often don't have the right information available to make decisions anyway. They call this the "limited rationality" of career decision making. They profess that, since uncertainty is real, we ought to be positive about it and begin to become more creative in our decision making.

The Gelatts believe that there are four paradoxical principles to positive uncertainty (p. 6). These can be taken in any order.

1. Be focused and flexible about what you want.

   Focus and flexibility are going to help you to continue to discover and create new goals over the course of your educational and career path. They also promote the idea that what you have as goals for today may not be the ones that you have for tomorrow. I've often told my students that my own definition of mental health could be summed up in one word, "flexibility." And mental illness could be defined as trying the same failing tactics over and over again without success. Having the family understand the need for flexibility would be a challenging but useful task, especially if they reflected on other family members who had taken creative risks.

2. Be aware and wary of what you know.

With technical changes, most have become painfully aware of what they don't know. I need neighborhood teens to help me with any computer glitches. But what may make matters worse is that the skills you have today may not be the ones you need tomorrow. And material that you do know will probably become obsolete in a short period of time anyway. My clients have often asked what they should look for in a job; and I've said one thing. "What will you learn on the job? What new skills will you obtain? If you're not going to learn anything new when you leave one job for another, which you will inevitably do, you will be a generation behind if you haven't kept up with the advances, especially technical advances, in the work world. Family members who maintain a rigid stance need to consider this.

3. Be realistic and optimistic about what you believe.

As I pointed out earlier (Chope, 2000), beliefs are enormously powerful. Theologians have focused upon beliefs for time immemorial. Beliefs, whether based upon strong data, scant data, or spiritual leanings, are driving forces in our decision making. People invest in the stock market based upon what they believe to be true about the future of a particular organization. The belief in the dot coms drove the NASDAQ to record heights. We form beliefs about ourselves, our environment, and the way that we as individuals interact with our environment.

4. Be practical and magical about what you do.

This is the place where the Gelatts suggest that you use both your head and your heart when making decisions. But they emphasize that the choices are still left up to the individual. It is in this area that the focus turns away from intelligence and more toward intuition. It is here that we are encouraged to see the bigger picture that can fill us with passion and excitement. The once and future king of Apple Computer, Steve Jobs, didn't just construct and assemble computers. In the late 1990s, he noticed the impending revolution in digital music and ended up creating the groundbreaking iPod. What a wonderful combination of the practical and magical, a story for every family to hear.

The Gelatts suggest that rationality be tempered by looking for greater possibilities. In the earlier paper, Gelatt (1989) had several recommendations for how to accomplish this: redefine success, embrace change, and find new partnerships. The family ought to consider these as well.

Redefine Success. First, career decision makers ought to redefine success. They should know that the career ladder will not be linear, but will be more like a matrix. I've found that in the latest career moves my clients engage more in work projects and less in career jobs. Organizations hire people for a period to successfully complete what is needed, and then they will move either to a new project or out of the organization. So people need to manage their careers differently. In surviving in this career world, people will need to be more fluid, less rigid, and certainly more creative.

For clients entering new jobs where many have said "don't take a downgrade," I've suggested they actually aim lower. You can begin almost anywhere in an organization and move around some before trying to move up. Gathering new skills and knowledge along with meeting people will be the greatest assets that any organization can give to a worker. Organizations change their structures regularly, worrying about hierarchical organizational reporting charts stifles creativity and the searching for new possibilities. Maneuverability is the key to success.

Embrace Change. Embracing change will force people to go beyond merely accepting that change and instability are inevitable. In only one year, there is more information available than was available for the entire lifetime of people from just two generations ago. So, absorbing new ideas and concepts are essential. And, with a positive outlook about change, there will be ample opportunities to become more creative by becoming more imaginative. In such a short time, we have evolved from the car phone to the cell phone to video phones to video phones with text messaging that can connect to the Internet. This is due to people embracing change and creating new possibilities.

Find New Partnerships. In both happenstance and positive uncertainty, staying connected is essential for decision makers. Making new friends and colleagues through networks that include work, professional organizations, clubs, and hobbies are an important ingredient in this process. There are ways that new information can be shared to create new opportunities, and that is what the decision maker needs to be on the lookout for. Connecting a cell phone to the Internet is just one example of a recently developed new partnership.

Career Self-Efficacy

The last method of decision making included here has both rational and nonrational components. It is based upon the work of Bandura (1977) that was later expanded upon by Betz and Hackett (1981). Self-efficacy expectations can drive your decision making. It's the attitude that you have regarding your capacity to successfully perform demanding behaviors. Your expectation of how successful you'll be often determines whether or not you'll take the risk and solidify a career decision. Efficacy expectations will influence career choices as well as your success on a job.

According to Bandura there are four sources of information that affect career decision self-efficacy:

1. Performance accomplishments
2. Vicarious learning or modeling
3. Verbal persuasion and encouragement from others important to you
4. High level of arousal. A little arousal is needed to be most efficacious, but too much results in nervousness and inefficiency

In making decisions, you can focus on each of the areas. You can start by counting your accomplishments. That's the raw material that makes up the foundation of how well you think you'll do in new situations. Significant accomplishments deserve to be recognized with pride. You can list your accomplishments and then try to see which ones best represent the transferable skills that you have developed. You can even have other members of your family help you with this exercise. Sometimes, significant others are aware of special skills you have that you don't evaluate as very special. Analyzing your accomplishments can help you to increase the expectations that you have for yourself.

You can experience vicarious learning in a number of ways. In the career decision making process, it's often useful to read biographies of others and how they made the career decisions that they did. Instead of reading, you can model the behavior of people that you admire, assuming or imitating some of the activities that they engage in either on the job or in social circumstances. And you can try job shadowing, spending extended periods of time with someone and watching how they perform their job tasks.

Of course, to be most efficacious, you need some encouragement from others, a rooting section, if you will. If family members are not going to be encouraging, then you'll need to find others who will be. Everybody can have their behavior shaped by positive feedback; behaviorists have known this for years. Two techniques are useful for this. The first is to make a list of all of the encouraging messages that you've had in the past. And make a list of the people who have been encouraging toward you and also the ones that you have been encouraging towards. Second, if you can't list enough positive support, then create a group of significant others in your own mind and develop scripts for each of them. What would they say about you that is overwhelmingly positive about your personal attributes? How would this information help with your career decision making? If these ideas don't work and you're questioning your self-esteem, consider a support group on a campus or in the community to be a ready-made cheering section.

Finally, keep your energy up. Don't get too high or too low in the process. There is an optimal level of energy to the process that is important to maintain.

Chapter Summary

So, to conclude the material on decision making, it's important to know that there are rational and nonrational approaches to the process. Your intuition and family culture as well as your spirituality can contribute to deciding what process is best for you to use. By understanding your decision making style, you can suggest to your family members ways that they can contribute to your efforts. Many of these decision making strategies can assist you or others in the process of breaking away from a stranglehold of family beliefs and attitudes.

Chapter 6

Out of the Home and into the Classroom

"Education is what survives when what has been
learned has been forgotten."
B.F. Skinner

Since I've been on the bandwagon about incorporating families
into career counseling classes, this chapter is presented for
educators, trainers, and consultants. It will, of course, also be of
interest to lay readers. The topics suggested for the classroom
include professional standards, case studies, biographies, guided
autobiographies, genograms, family systems theory, family
sculpting, and psychodrama. Material discussing how counselors
can work with parents of school age children is also considered
and the literature reviewed.

As promoted throughout the book, most career counselors are given
only scant information about material related to family influence in career
decision making in the course of their graduate education. And the family
therapy courses that are offered as a part of a 60-unit master's program in
career or college counseling are usually devoted to broadly based family
therapy issues that, when taught, appear to be disconnected from career
counseling.

That is certainly unfortunate because choices people make about
their careers surely influence family dynamics. Job loss generally results
in depression and sometimes even suicide; suicide rates and unemployment
rates have been known to rise and fall together. Conflicts about work
overflow into family life; there are conceivably more marital breakups as
a result of these conflicts than there are over marital infidelity. And, of
course, people will uproot their family and move to a different geographical
location if it appears that the move will be for better work opportunities.

Of course, career change is inevitable for everyone; even good
changes will be stressful for many. Ten years ago, career counselors
thought that people would go through five or six major career changes in
their lives. The current thoughts among seasoned professionals is that it

will be more like seven or eight. All these changes will take place in the context of family and other relationship issues. Blustein (2001) has emphasized that these work and relationship issues, which include social and instrumental support, are quite complicated and multidimensional. And he notes further that there remains very little *empirical* evidence that allows for an understanding of the overlap between work and relationships. It really has been, up until now, an area that has been left without extensive research and scholarship. So, there's no obvious body of information readily available to easily integrate into graduate level counseling courses except for the bits and pieces of research summarized in Chapter 2.

This poses a dilemma for counselor educators attempting to introduce new family-related material into course curricula. Clearly, this text has pointed to some useful points on the influence of the family in the career decision making process. But this begs the question as to what type of instructional material counselor educators should add to their courses. And how can educators ensure that their fledging counselors are appropriately trained to seek out and address the family components of career decision making?

Previous Attempts

To some extent, bringing family and personal relationship material into career counseling classes has been both complicated and frustrating. Nevertheless, historically, different theorists and writers have given more than lip service to the intertwining of career, personal, and family issues. Researchers have added the context of relationships in their approaches to career counseling. For example, in their 1973 model, Gysbers and Moore (1973) defined life career development as self-development over the life span through a process of interaction and accompanying integration of a person's life roles, life settings, and life events. This was an honest attempt at creating a holistic approach to career decision making.

This work was expanded upon by McDaniels and Gysbers (1992) with the addition of factors of race, gender, and ethnic origin, along with religious beliefs to assist in understanding how these factors influenced an individual's perception of career choice, career roles, work settings and life events. And, more recently, the religious factor has been enhanced to reflect the incorporation of spirituality into the career decision making process. Meanwhile, sexual orientation has been added as a new factor to the 1992 expansion. Socioeconomic status, another factor from the original conceptualization, has been changed to social class (Gysbers, Heppner, & Johnston, 2003).

The pivotal research described in Chapter 2, provided Blustein's

(2001) thoughtful summary of the literature on the interface between relationships and work. He focused upon the existential question of how behavior in one domain, like family, will affect behavior in another domain, like work. Other research has addressed family systems or attachment theory, both of which are important, although more study is needed.

Much of the information about family influence on career choice is anecdotal or taken from case material later reported upon by practitioners. But the amount and kind of evidence on how families affected career decisions is regularly illustrated in the public press.

Take professional baseball players, for example, who break the education mold and, unlike most, have college degrees. They do so because of family influences. John Shea (2004) prepared a study on the number of college graduates in Major League Baseball. Interestingly, only 42 of the 750 active, non-disabled list players had college degrees. This is in stark contrast to professional football. In fact, the Carolina Panthers of the National Football League had 43 college graduates, more than all of Major League Baseball! Who are some of these exceptions? Eric Karros was one of two players on the Oakland Athletics to have a college degree. His was in economics from UCLA. When asked about why he finished his degree, Karros explained that academics were an important part of his family experience. His mother was a graduate of San Diego State University while his father had a degree from Yale. Karros had gone to UCLA for the academics, but became a walk-on baseball player while attending classes. He persuaded the baseball coach for a tryout.

Brian Dallimore from the San Francisco Giants is one course away from his psychology degree from Stanford. He reportedly feels pressure from his family to finish his education and has announced publicly that his family would insist that he complete his degree. Stanford baseball coach, Mark Marquess, believes that it is truly sinful for parents to send a child for a Stanford education for three years and then not be able to watch the child graduate (Shea, 2004).

Still, there continues to be a struggle about how to add this contextual information into career courses in a way that can also be easily integrated into clinical work. In part, this has been due to two determinants. The first is a continuing fear that career counselors may be working beyond the scope of their practice by bringing in family and relationship issues. The second is that the individuals teaching family therapy classes that career counseling students typically attend usually have no exposure to career counseling. Many continue to believe that career counseling is notoriously dull and, in the end, not truly counseling.

How Professional Associations Address These Issues

The professional associations that govern and establish standards for career counselors have developed a framework for the type of information that should be taught in classes devoted to this specialization. I'd like to begin with a review of two sets of guidelines. Counselor educators, students, practitioners, and clients should be aware of these guidelines. Therefore, they should be covered in the course material of at least one class devoted to career counseling. The first set is the Career Counseling Competencies of the National Career Development Association (NCDA, 1997). And the second set is the published standards of the Counsel on The Accreditation of Counseling and Related Educational Programs (CACREP), the accrediting body of the American Counseling Association.

Career Counseling Competencies

There are 12 sections of the NCDA Competencies that are intended to be representative of the minimum competencies that a career professional should possess at the master's level and above. The competencies are a result of the work of the NCDA Professional Standards Committee and are reviewed by the Committee, NCDA Board, and other relevant associations when deemed appropriate.

The following list includes the competencies related to family influence that the NCDA Professional Standards Committee believes represents minimum competencies. The three sections that include family material or contextual material related to families are listed below along with the specific numerical subsections that speak to the skills, knowledge, or awareness that demonstrates competency.

Career Development Theory

Theory base and knowledge considered essential for professionals engaging in career counseling and development. Demonstration of knowledge of:

Subsection 6. Role relationships that facilitate life-work planning
Individual and Group Counseling Skills
Individual and group counseling competencies considered essential to effective career counseling. Demonstration of ability to:

> **Subsection 6.** Identify and understand social contextual conditions affecting clients' careers.
>
> **Subsection 7.** Identify and understand familial, sub-cultural, and cultural structures and functions as they are related to clients' careers.
>
> **Subsection 8.** Identify and understand clients' career decision making processes.

Information Resources

Information/resource base and knowledge essential for professionals engaging in career counseling. Demonstration of knowledge of:

> **Subsection 4.** Changing roles of women and men and the implications that this has for education, family, and leisure.

The text has offered and described a variety of techniques and assessment devices that can be used to study the influence of the family on career decision making. These can be used to demonstrate the relationship and contextual variables like family interaction patterns and childrearing patterns that affect later career decision making. This material and exercises should be added to courses in career counseling and related courses to more completely meet the NCDA standards. Understanding changing roles and relationships with others is perceived as enormously important by NCDA.

The 2001 CACREP Standards are divided into generic sections which cover the following: The Institution, Program Objectives and Curriculum, Clinical Instruction, Faculty and Staff, Organization and Administration, Evaluations in the Programs. In the generic standards for all counselors, there is the expectation that everyone will have some knowledge of career development and, furthermore, that they will learn about the relational aspects of career development. The specific language is given below.

Program Objectives and Curriculum

> **Subsection K.** Curricular experiences and demonstrated knowledge in each of eight common core areas are required of all students in the program.
>
> > **Core Area 4.** Career Development studies that provide an understanding of career development and related life factors, including all of the following:

> **Subsection d.** Interrelationships among and between work, family, and other life roles and factors including the role of diversity and gender in career development

Curiously, the 2001 CACREP Standards for the accreditation of career counseling programs are quite limited regarding curricular standards and family influence. The Standards indicate that besides common core experiences that are outlined above in Section II.k.4.d. for all counselors, there are particular curricular experiences and demonstrated knowledge and skills that are required of all of the students in a career counseling program. These are articulated under the Standards for Career Counseling Programs, Section A.6.

This section points to one area of the "curricular experiences and demonstrated knowledge and skills" and demands exposure to "the role of racial, ethnic, and cultural heritage, nationality, socioeconomic status, family structure, age, gender, sexual orientation, religious and spiritual beliefs, occupations, and physical and mental status, and equity issues in career counseling" (CACREP, 2001).

Based upon the aforementioned NCDA Competencies and 2001 CACREP Standards, I've proposed the following recommendations that should be considered in developing course work for students in career counseling as well as general counseling.

Useful Published Case Material

Since our goal is to understand a wide range of contextual factors, career counseling classes can be well served by using published cases from the career development literature. Cases in the literature can be used for demonstration purposes and lend themselves to class discussion. Even material that isn't necessarily focused upon family influence can still assist in leading to speculation about what contextual variables may have influenced a particular career decision.

Between 1986 and 1993, there was a section of the *Career Development Quarterly (CDQ)*, the journal of the NCDA, titled "Getting Down to Cases" which offered 19 separate cases. These were career counseling case narratives presented and then subsequently commented upon by two or three practicing counselors or counselor educators. Blustein et al. (2001) point out that the cases provided a variety of different counseling issues for discussion and reflection. These issues included some that were quite complex, like career indecision and adjustment to disabling conditions.

"Getting Down to Cases" should be required reading for educators and students who are in need of case material for career counseling classes. The case material provides an opportunity for a further explication of the influence of family members in career decision making while adding to the more complex material of the interconnections between work and other relationships.

Blustein et al. (2001) analyzed the 19 cases to "identify themes pertaining to overlap between work and interpersonal relationships" (p. 240). They whet the appetite for more analysis of these kinds of data to legitimize the study of the interrelationship of careers with other family and contextual issues. To be fair, Blustein et al. did not only explore the family of origin in their attempt to understand the intersection between work and relationships. They studied a variety of roles that were influenced by the family. But they did note in their analysis how they and other researchers have witnessed intriguing behavior of people who replay roles within their families in their workplace situations.

In previous research, Yalom (1995) has pointed out this same type of behavior by observing family of origin issues in group therapy. One of his primary factors is called the "corrective recapitulation of the primary family group" (p.13), and he notes that the therapy group resembles in many ways the family of origin. In perhaps a similar vein, the work experience can resemble the family of origin. The workplace allows for many different peer relationships, along with the presence of authority figures, a pervasive sense of competition, anger, and hostility at rejection, and, perhaps for some, disappointment at not being the most loved and most respected person in the facility.

Blustein et al. (2001) focused upon four themes in their analysis of the manner in which work and nonwork factors intersect: relational support, motivational and conflicted themes, recapitulation of family roles, and social and economic frame. Interestingly and to their disappointment, they admit that they could not determine any notable trends in 50% of the cases. Regardless, the classification of the case material that they were able to make serves as a useful model for continuing this work in classroom settings as well as in future research efforts.

Exemplifying relational support, they describe an African-American client who wants to make her mother proud, a laundromat employee who receives encouragement and support from his uncle and fiancé, and a doctoral student who has little support from his family and lives with a spouse who can be at once both demanding and supportive. Motivational problems are described with a college graduate who moved home and was pressured by her parents to become more independent, while judgmental about her relationship with an older man. And the importance of family roles is illustrated with the case of a client who seeks parental approval for all of her major life decisions.

Family influences certainly interface with economic factors as clients struggle to adjust to the impact of major changes on their lifestyle because of changes in work demands and work hours. Clearly, some family obligations may "contribute to remaining in an unsatisfying job, remaining underemployed, and/or, limiting one's career dreams" (p. 253). And, to be sure, for those who suffer from some form of disability or impairment, family support can be the key to maneuvering through the career world.

Personal Acquaintances

Reading the material that has summarized the *CDG*, "Getting Down to Cases," students can be encouraged to find examples in other sectors that explore, in some depth, the intersection between work and family. Assignments can be developed from the career counseling literature, but personal stories that people share can be remarkably useful in the classroom.

One of my college classmates was Hal Krents, who was told at the age of nine that he would be totally blind. Still, with the strong and regular support of his family, he was able to graduate from Harvard College and Law School. He authored a book about his life called *To Race the Wind* (Krents, 1972); and the curious experiences with his draft board became the inspiration for the Broadway play and later movie, *Butterflies Are Free*. He describes in his autobiography the consistent support he had from his family in pursuing his life goals. Although he died an untimely death, he was a specialist in rehabilitation law and influential in the passage of the Rehabilitation Act of 1973. He also served as a member of the President's Committee on Employment of the Handicapped.

The most useful information about family influences and career choices come from stories all around us. For example, lessons can be learned from the lives of politicians and other well known people.

Biographies of People in Politics

There is probably no substitute for understanding the role of the influence of the family than to ferret out the information from biographies of well-known people who choose to write about their parents.

Joseph Wilson

In 2004, former ambassador Joseph Wilson wrote a book about the headline-making scandal of his wife's CIA cover being revealed in national newspapers. The book, titled *The Politics of Truth: Inside the Lies that Led to War and Betrayed My Wife's CIA Identity: A Diplomat's Memoir* (Wilson, 2004), was partly autobiographical and gave revealing information about his life and his path into politics. Like other politicians, Wilson had a famous ancestor, according to Heidi Benson (2004). That would be "Sunny Jim" Rolph, the mayor of San Francisco from 1912 until 1931. Rolph later became the Republican governor of California until his death in 1934.

Wilson writes that he grew up knowing that his relative always was dressed in a cowboy hat and carnation. He built the magnificent City Hall and was the person behind the placement of Father Junipero's statue in Statuary Hall in Washington. Wilson grew up in a family that had a history of political and public service to the country. In the 1960s, however, Wilson's parents, who had been World War II military personnel, moved to Europe, where Wilson attended high school and learned to surf and ski. He matriculated at the University of California at Santa Barbara, graduating in 1972, then worked as a carpenter building homes in California and later Washington State. But the rain and generally poor weather in the northwest drove him back to school where he studied international relations and economics at the University of Washington. Fluent in French and with a strong international perspective, he took and passed the demanding Foreign Service exam on what he called a whim. In 1976, the former surfer and carpenter, followed the family tradition and became a diplomat. He was the last American official to meet with Saddam Hussein before the beginning of the first Gulf War.

American Presidents

American presidents become interesting material for studying family influence. According to Pika, Maltese, & Thomas (2002), five American families produced 10 American presidents. The Adams had a father and son as did the Bushes. James Madison and Zachary Taylor had grandparents in common while William Henry Harrison was grandfather to Benjamin Harrison. Theodore and Franklin Roosevelt were cousins. Of course, John Kennedy's father, Joseph Kennedy, was the chairman of the Securities and Exchange Commission and also ambassador to Great Britain; and Joseph's sons, Robert and Ted Kennedy, were senators and both sought the presidency. Many of the Kennedy grandchildren have run for political office in Rhode Island, Massachusetts, and Maryland. President Pierce's father was governor of New Hampshire; and Prescott Bush, father of George and grandfather of George W., was a senator from

Connecticut. Al Gore's father was a senator as well. The list goes on, but you can see the point.

There are, of course, cases among the presidents where the influence is less obvious. This is much like what Blustein et al. (2001) found in the analysis of the *CDQ* cases. For example, Eisenhower, Nixon, and Reagan were all sons of poor men who had spotty employment records. The fathers of Johnson, Ford, and Carter had only tepid success in business. But Pika et al. (2002) comment that, in the studies of American presidents, it seems that most achieved "political success with a substantial boost from their family circumstances, advantages that included political and social standing as well as educational and professional opportunities unavailable to most of their fellow citizens" (p. 136).

Lyndon Baines Johnson

Lyndon Johnson is a particularly interesting case study from a career development perspective. Johnson's father, Sam, was a state legislator and a successor to Joseph Baines, the father of his wife, Rebekah Baines, in the position. According to James Barber (1992), Sam was a doer and a go-getter trying to out-perform all others in his work in the Capitol. Even though Sam had a checkered employment history as a teacher, rancher, real estate agent, and politician, he was extremely competitive and thought to be as "stubborn as a mule." On the marriage, people said that the Baines had the brains and the Johnsons had the guts (Barber, 1992, p.111).

Sam Johnson was sorry that they had little income from his work as a legislator and from debts he had accumulated in his cotton business. He had to leave the legislature in 1907 when he was married and returned in 1918 when Lyndon was 11. Lyndon soaked in what was happening around him. When the Texas governor was impeached, Lyndon watched as his own uncle served as the chief defense counsel. And Lyndon campaigned with his father. He listened to home spun stories and witnessed his father deliver patronage. His father warned him, "If you can't come into a roomful of people and tell right away who is for you and who is against you, you have no business in politics" (Barber, 1992, p.114). Lyndon would attend legislative sessions with his father and watch as deals were made regarding oil, beer, and the Ku Klux Klan.

His mother, Rebekah, also ensured that Lyndon would succeed. She wanted to make him a genius, reading to him endlessly and making sure that he had music and dancing lessons. She even coached him in debate. His father told him tales of his relatives from the Alamo and took him there as well as on the campaign trail. Classmates knew of Lyndon's ambition and, at his high school graduation at 15, the class believed that he would one day become the governor of Texas. While his life after high school was filled with turmoil, running away, and taking menial jobs, his mother insisted he go to college. When he finally decided to go to college, his mother pulled the necessary strings to get him into Southwest Texas State Teachers College in San Marcos. According to Berber (1992), his mother was also a dominating force, probably unnecessarily dominating. Yet, without her persuasive efforts and pressing on, he would certainly not have attended college and been put onto the path that took him to the Oval Office as the 36th president of the United States.

The review of well-known individuals and their family histories can prove to be terrific anecdotal information. For those who might be interested in a more personal undertaking, the guided autobiography might prove to be a useful endeavor.

Guided Autobiography

The increasing sensitivity to family issues in the career development process leads to the offering of a new technique not unlike that which was offered earlier in the context of narrative and contextual approaches to counseling. The Guided Autobiography (deVries, Birren, & Deutchman, 1995, 1990) has proven to be a useful technique that can be offered in career counseling classes or in job clubs for job seekers and changers. This is, according to the developers, an approach to life review that is geared to topics. It helps individuals place the vicissitudes of life in some perspective while it can provide anecdotal, ideographic evidence of the capacity that people have to address the challenges of life while finding and establishing their own sense of personal or vocational identity.

The Guided Autobiography is contained in two stages. The first stage is the writing of autobiographical essays on particular topics that each member of a group or job club or class can do individually. In the second stage, members read their topical autobiographical work to the group. Each topic is given a limit of two pages. The process has the effect of allowing each member to engage in his or her own personal exploration and then to receive feedback that enhances the experience of being in the group while also receiving feedback from the members that can assist in the career search process.

In the Guided Autobiography, participants typically meet nine or ten times for one- and one-half to two hours on each occasion. Depending upon the setting, whether at work, at school, or at an office, the process can be completed over the course of 2 weeks with daily meetings. However, it's possible to also meet weekly over the course of 9 or 10 weeks. Each group has 5 to 6 participants, which seems to work best for this process. Larger groups can be subdivided. Typically the group is a closed one so that new members are not added after the first meeting. The first group begins with the listing of 10 words by each member that characteristically describes who they are and then the 3 most frequently mentioned attributions are singled out. After finishing, the members share their lists and discuss the impact of these descriptors. Those who have difficulty with the activity can be asked to name an animal they resemble or a color they identify with.

At the first meeting, a theme is drawn from the following list: (a) major branching points in life, (b) family issues, (c) career choices, (d) the meaning of money, (e) health and body image (f) love and hate, (g) sexual identity, sexual roles and experiences, (h) experiences with death, and (i) aspirations and life goals and the meaning of life (deVries, et al., 1990, p.5). The group members are then asked to prepare an autobiographical essay of two pages that speaks to the theme.

At each of the subsequent meetings, a different theme is selected by the leaders.

The family-related themes can be easily restructured to reflect career problems and decisions for a job club, a career development class, or a group at a university career or counseling center. Brian deVries et al. (1995) point out that the use of themes prevents any unnecessary obsessing about particular events and instead expands a person's perspectives while helping individuals to maintain their focus. Nine, 2-page autobiographical essays might be written on the following themes: (a) role of parents' education on your career choice; (b) major life events of your family that affected career choice; (c) influence of parents' discussions on career choice; (d) influence of other relatives' experiences on career choice; (e) the role of money in the family; (f) the expectations of success in the family; (g) describing your first job to your parents or other relatives; (h) experience with telling your family about losing or quitting a job; and (i) aspirations or life goals to take from the group and how these fit into family expectations.

With these exercises, there is the potential for creating a new understanding of family roles and relationships and how they affect decision making. Sharing stories and listening to others helps to create a feeling within a career group of the universality of the experience of creating a career path and life identity. The material also lends itself to an exploration of the entire life span. The guided components of the work allow an opportunity for individuals to explore intergenerational communication with the family and, through the group process, to experience first-hand what it is like for other people to work with the material.

The Guided Autobiography is another in the genre of narrative approaches to understanding family and self. Yet it is particularly suited to classrooms as well as to job clubs and other consultation venues.

Besides the reading of original material that illustrates family influences, there can be a more academic study of a number of issues in career counseling classes or in the family therapy classes taken by some career counselors. The remainder of the chapter will suggest issues that could be a part of a career development class or family therapy class. These issues include: family systems, genograms, family sculpting, school-to-work transitions, social support, and ways parents can be assisted in being more helpful in their children's career planning.

Family Systems

There should be some course material in career development and other counseling programs that take into account family systems work. The family systems perspective allows for an understanding of social context and interaction patterns that demonstrate the interconnectedness between our family life and culture and the types of decisions that we make. For the career counselor, it allows for a perspective that gives a different standpoint to client attitudes about work rather than using traditional career development theory.

Many career decisions that people make are often difficult, not always because some of the solutions are unclear, but because family judgment is earnest and direct. For many current job seekers, there is terrific employment instability and they use the collective family wisdom for advice. A family systems perspective can help to analyze and understand how job seekers request and use family advice.

Family systems work can aid in understanding why people make some of their more questionable decisions. I am always amazed at the types of inappropriate decisions that many of my clients have made in the past. But, meandering through the histories of opinions and verdicts in the family, I have a better understanding, at least, of where they were coming from.

Clients from strong, achieving educational backgrounds have rebelled and made choices that were inconsistent with whom they really are. Others have had wildly inappropriate and unrealistic ideas of what they should be able to accomplish. I have had clients go bankrupt trying to emulate a parent. Some of the more severely abused clients are terribly indecisive and can't make choices. Others are negative about both their options and the choices they make, bordering upon depression; and still others can't seem to get along with their coworkers. In all of these cases, the very best understanding of the client's problems has come about by using a family systems perspective in the counseling.

Beth

There wasn't much that Beth couldn't do. She had done exceptionally well in school, earning two Master's degrees, one in business administration and another in journalism. She had hoped for a career in corporate communications, eventually being able to be the head of a communications or public relations department at a large multinational endeavor. She had her eyes on companies like General Electric and Proctor and Gamble. And she was ambitious.

Beth's career path never took off the way that she anticipated. Instead, she worked mostly as a contract worker or free-lancer, unable to secure full time work. She rarely applied for positions that were congruent with her education and skill level; and, the few times that she did, she quit within six months. She attributed her failures to the lack of opportunities or the fact of her being a woman or that the companies were filled with uncreative people who didn't know how to deal with her.

None of this was the case. Beth had come from a family with two older sisters who repeatedly told her that she would never amount to anything. Her mother concurred and worried that Beth wouldn't be able to function independently without some help. While the words of her mother were often encouraging, her mannerisms belied her voice. Her sisters, who married young and never worked, were forever critical of Beth.

It was only by using a family systems perspective that Beth could understand how her career path and ambition had gone off track. She came to understand that she was expected to fail, or at least not live up to her anticipated successes. According to family therapist Sal Minuchin (1974), Beth had learned to play a role in her life that kept the system in balance. Her two siblings and mother were dissatisfied with their lives and relationships with men. Beth even questioned why her mother married her father. With all of the unhappiness abounding, Beth was expected to also play a particular role filled with disappointment. She sought some refuge from her father, but he was unavailable to everyone.

Beth was enmeshed in a dysfunctional family system, filled with depressing judgments about her capacity for success. There was little healthy communication in the family. Satir and Baldwin (1983) have pointed out earlier how poor communication among family members can lead to a variety of emotional, relationship, and work-related problems.

Satir (1983) has suggested that communication problems occur when communication is incongruent, when what is said verbally is inconsistent with body postures, tone of voice, and facial expression. She has gone on to say (Satir, 1988) that there are patterns of dysfunctional communication in families. These communication patterns allow people to avoid their real feelings and perceptions. They can be exemplified in communications like placating (always saying yes), blaming (finding fault), computing (using only facts, devoid of feeling), and distracting (avoiding conflict or direct communication).

Basic communication problems like these need treatment according to family therapist Jay Haley (1991). In the career arenas, they result in people developing their own poor communication styles and then recreating the family system in their working relationships. That describes Beth. She was hypersensitive and couldn't trust her supervisors. These patterns can also result in people not being able or willing to acknowledge their own strengths and thereafter ending up in a pattern of indecisiveness about their career choice. With all of her academic accomplishments, Beth didn't feel that she counted for much. She remembers her mother referring to her as a "vocational eunuch." She recapitulated these thoughts in the workplace.

Career counselors would be well served by understanding the communication styles in the family, to know what the communication rules in the household were. They should also help clients to understand themselves as a part of a system. What were the roles that people played, how were problems solved, what types of boundaries existed between each member of the family, and what were the communication patterns? A general approach to family systems and family counseling with a systems perspective can be found in Kaplan (2003).

Genograms

While these have been mentioned earlier in the book, they should become a part of the material that is used in counselor education. There are many books on genograms and close to 8,000 genogram sites on the Internet, obtained by simply entering "genogram" into a browser like Internet Explorer.

Quite clearly, career decision making can be understood in the context of the family, and the genogram lays this out in a representative way that can be reviewed on a continuous basis. Counselor educators should be able to teach the purpose of the genogram and its administration, and then give typical examples of the genogram. Students should be given the opportunity to construct their own genograms and then engage in a personal analysis of the drawing. This can include the nature of decision making, use of power, political beliefs, expressions of anger, substance abuse, addictive behaviors, illnesses, catastrophic deaths, and emotional demands. When I request genograms from my clients or students, I ask that they be sure to note educational levels and careers that each member of the family had.

From these data, important information about the culture of the family and the impact that it had on an individual's career decision making process can be had. The genogram information allows for a continuing exploration of family history and the themes that seem to encompass the family. Savickas (1995) looks for stories in a genogram and has clients discover the heroes and heroines in the family. And it has been noted by Kuehl (1995) that clients feel heard when their career issues are connected to some type of relational context.

Papp and Imber-Black (1996) have developed a clever technique that uses the genogram to discover family themes and facilitate change. They believe that when the genogram is constructed, themes and beliefs about the family and cultures can be made evident and then traced intergenerationally. They suggest the following questions and guidelines for the counselor to follow in this process of discovery (pp. 18-19).

1. What are some of the beliefs or attitudes held by family members that have an impact on the presenting problem?
2. What is the daily interactional pattern that takes place in response to these beliefs, and what is the central theme that emerges from this pattern?
3. Using the genogram, ask theme oriented questions and look for repetitions of the theme intergenerationally.
4. Observe how the theme is carried out in contexts outside of the family.
5. Design a set of questions that alter or challenge the theme.
6. Think about possible interventions to address the theme.

There are, in each of the genogram drawings, patterns that emerge that are fascinating. I have noticed a tradition of sailing in my own family genogram. I hail from a line of ship captains and sailors and it seems as if half of the 100 or so people in my extended family live around water and own a boat. One cousin is a lawyer who represents a great lakes freighter shipping company. My extended family of aunts, uncles, and cousins are all boat owners, and each has maintained a legacy of power boat ownership. My father and I were the only sailboat owners among the very large family. Yet the boating themes were elements of adventure, strength, risk taking, strategy, and collegiality. And when people have asked me to speak to my ability to take risks or to manage a team, I reflect on my racing days on San Francisco Bay with strong tides, thirty-knot winds, and large ocean swells.

Genograms can be shared as a group activity and can serve as an ice breaker in workshops, career classes, and in personal activities. As mentioned earlier, I ask each of my clients to prepare a career genogram before their first visit to my office. And, with this, they have already begun to explore why they made some of the decisions that they did.

The Family Sculpture and Other Techniques from Psychodrama

Themes that emerge from the genogram can be used by different groups of people in staging a type of psychodrama called family sculpting or "sculpting" (Gladding, 1995). In this technique, a single group member becomes the protagonist and arranges a small group of people from a class or large group into a configuration that resembles his or her family in a particular setting that might exist in the home. Eating a meal, having a discussion, attending a party together, or just standing around are common examples. The individuals in the sculpture are asked to assume roles and then are given guidance by the protagonist to assume particular body postures and facial expressions. One of the members also plays the role of the protagonist in the family sculpture. The work is all done nonverbally except for the guidance from the protagonist. Each member of a group can be given a chance to create a sculpture of his or her family. With each of the sculptures, family themes can be discussed.

In my counseling experience, one of the most common sculptures pictures the protagonist with the family when the protagonist announces upsetting news. Choosing a college major or degree that is out-of-sorts with the authority figures in the family always makes for an interesting sculpture.

This technique can be used to assist others in addressing not only family members, but other authority figures and coworkers with whom a person may be in some conflict. In any event, a student as a protagonist could share a genogram and then describe what was most difficult in announcing their career decision to the family. The student could pick other members of the class and give a family role to each member. Then, in the configuration, the student can tell each person how the family member looked. This allows the student to see the family as an outside observer. They can get feedback from others who are either participating or are observing the experience.

I have also found that it can be useful to have a student or a group member as protagonist give a soliloquy about how one or both parents reacted to their career choice. Sometimes, people act out the words and phrases that they obsess upon when they think about how their family members will react to some of their own choices. The remainder of the class or group can then react to the soliloquy as a type of Greek chorus.

There is also a Gestalt technique referred to as the monodrama where a protagonist can play all of the parts of the dialogue between themselves and their parents, including the internal thoughts that they have while acting out the experience (Gladding, 1995). And, of course, there can be the use of the role reversal, where the protagonist plays the antagonist role—like the father—while their real life role is played by another student or group member.

This type of work helps the students and other group members learn about family dynamics in the here and now and to witness some of the conflicts that people go through as they try to create a path that may be different from the one that their parents had hoped they would play. These techniques support thinking on the feet and becoming creative in responding to others. Feedback from others who are actors in the dramas or members of the Greek chorus can help a protagonist to clarify his or her feelings about the career issues being contended with.

The Transition from School to Work

The school-to-work transition is often an area that receives little attention in either career or school counseling programs. Many career theories and the attitudes of career professionals take the position that career counseling is geared more toward a professionally minded clientele and not to the noncollege-bound youth of America. The irony of this is that Frank Parsons (1909) placed much of his theoretical and practical approaches to helping impoverished youths transition from school-to-work. Yet, with regard to the decision making of youth who are not college bound, understanding the decision making abilities of this group and the influence and support of their families is enormously important. It has been recommended already that there is a need for vocational psychologists to develop new theories for a population of noncollege-bound youth that will serve to understand the contextual variables that influence their career decision making (Worthington & Juntunen, 1997).

There needs to be a continuing elaboration and discussion of issues that emerge between school counselors and career counselors. School counselors deal directly with parents, the influential members of a context that represents economics, ethnicity, class, and spirituality. Career counselors provide services which assist individuals in developing their own human capital in order to survive in an increasingly complex world. But school and career counselors don't often talk to each other. There are increasing examples shown by Solberg et al. (2002) that demonstrate the need to increase collaborations between counselor training programs and school districts to promote the career and personal development of students.

Blustein (1995) has suggested that there will need to be more emphasis on the contextual variables that affect the noncollege-bound youth. This work will have a new focus on issues like economics, sociological variables, social psychological variables, and the like. All of the noncollege, vocationally bound, like the politicians and presidents described earlier, have made decisions based in part upon family influence. In addition, there will be a greater need to attend to familial issues of diversity regarding this group as they will not represent the still predominantly white upper crusts of society that typically attend college and enter professional positions.

Students under the School-To-Work Opportunities Act of 1994 will benefit from assistance in developing decision making skills, visualizing greater career and work options, and learning about educational, apprenticeship and on-the-job training resources. Consultation with parents can be an integral part of this process and counselors and psychologists can work in partnership with students and parents to provide information about the career decision making process. Knowing the influence of the family in career decision making can only help to motivate counselors to enlist the power of the family in providing many of the support vehicles mentioned earlier in the text. It appears that engendering motivation of these students and confronting apathy and discouragement will be the most important work of the service providers. Having parents see the possibilities is perhaps the most important offering that can be made. We will want to have them involved in career exploration programs so that they are able to provide information that will increase positive outcomes. With immigrant families, we will want to be in the position of describing and promoting options.

Blustein et al. (1997) offered ten propositions based upon their research in developing approaches to address the needs of vocationally bound youth. Two of the propositions, numbers 4 and 9, directly relate to the influences of family in career decisions. They emphasize the importance of instructional support and relational context. Proposition 4 states that "Young adults who use their indigenous relational supports in making career decisions by obtaining support, advice, and consultation from others are more likely to negotiate transitions from school to work"

(p. 391). Proposition 9 states that "The experience of close relationships that are characterized by emotional and instrumental support in conjunction with challenging interpersonal opportunities provides young adults with an optimal relational context to support their transition from school to work" (p. 394). And, they recognize the importance of families when they conclude that "the transition to work seems to function most optimally when families, significant others, and counselors are available to assist both instrumentally and emotionally" (p. 394). These generalizations emerge from research. They reinforce for us the importance of the relational experience in determining a career purpose and direction regardless of education.

Career educators can assign projects for students to continue to explore the relational contexts in the school-to-work transition. Educators might have students explore how positive mentoring and family influence assists at-risk youth in becoming more reliant in overcoming barriers to employment or career development. This could investigate how positive outcomes are related to social support.

Positive Outcomes and Social Support

What are the factors that influence self-esteem with regard to work? Schultheiss, Kress, Manzi, and Glasscock (2001) have pointed out that there are demonstrated interconnections between our relationships and work lives. They add that the strongest factor of relational influence was support from the family, including the parents and siblings. Their findings are consistent with Bowlby (1982). Schultheiss et al. (2001) organized the concept of support into five functions: emotional support, social integration or network support, esteem support, information support, and tangible assistance.

Emotional support was defined as a factor of basic encouragement while *social integration* exemplified the feeling or connectedness that people experience when they hold common histories and personal characteristics.

Esteem support was characterized as a form of encouragement and a sense of pushiness by the parents to have their offspring live up to certain potentials.

Information support was perceived as the provision of facts about the work world.

And finally, *tangible assistance* was defined as helping with particular tasks or providing helpful resources. Obviously money was the most potent of these influences.

In a similar vein, Blustein, et al. (2001), in their exploration of the 19 cases previously mentioned from the *CDQ,* found that relationships with family members and friends provided emotional support in addressing particular career development tasks. They also found that a lack of a family support could have a deleterious effect on career decision making. To be sure, however, the picture is, according to Blustein et al. (1997), somewhat more complex than simply an endorsement of emotional support. They point out ironically that close sibling relationships can have a deleterious influence on the job satisfaction of some. This might be due to youth culture of today, sibling rivalry, competition, or family enmeshment among other possibilities. Like Schultheiss et al. (2001), they also show that emotional support is not the only ingredient in relational support. Instrumental support, or the degree to which support is manifested in activities like suggesting job possibilities, locating positions, and imparting useful information about the work world is, also, a significant contribution.

Helping Parents and Other Family Members to Become More Appropriate

Parenting style is, in large measure, responsible for the overall healthy functioning of the family. And parental involvement in the career planning process is undoubtedly critical to providing both the instrumental and emotional support necessary for adolescents to develop a sense of themselves in the world of work.

Kenny and Donaldson (1992) found that positive parental attachment was associated with better academic and personal adjustment in traditionally aged first-year college women. Dorgu (1994) found that when parents participated in school activities like homework and the PTA (Parent Teachers Association), there was an improvement in the achievement level of the student.

Educators need to begin to create models that will bring counselors into the dialogue with parents and children. Counselors will need to be taught techniques that will allow them to interact equally as effectively with parents and with students.

Chapter Summary

In this chapter there has been a focus on the activities that can be used by educators, trainers and group leaders to bring the experience and study of family influence into the classroom. There is a great deal of work that needs to be accomplished among counselor educators to ensure that the important variable of family influence is made a part of the training program for career counselors. A variety of techniques are available for classes in both career counseling and family therapy. Narratives, biographies, genograms, family systems, family sculpting, and Gestalt therapy have been mentioned. These classes can also create the atmosphere for more substantial discussions between career counselors and school counselors to empower parents to work more closely with school districts in building students' self-esteem while enhancing their opportunities for satisfying career choices.

Chapter 7

Looking to the Future

"Work is love made visible and if you cannot work with love but only with distaste, it is better that you should leave your work and sit at the gates of the temple and take alms of those who work with joy."
Kahlil Gibran

This chapter completes the book with some cautions for the future. It then offers some survival tips for jobs seekers, demonstrating how the family can be used in an upbeat way to support various career and educational decisions. These tips include having help in making decisions, building a community of support, creating a portfolio career, and considering being a "walk on." The chapter also emphasizes the importance of mattering, a theme that has echoed throughout the pages of the book.

As demonstrated throughout the book, families influence our careers and career choices. This is illustrated in our own lives and in the lives of well-known actors, authors, politicians, and athletes.

It's useful to ask what will be in store for us in the future, where families, as we have understood them, will be so very different. The nuclear family consisting of a stay-at-home spouse may near extinction. There's a high probability that some parents today, for a variety of health-related issues, will outlive their children. This will impact caregiving and attitudes that parents and children have about their careers and career choices.

Turbulence Will Continue

Many people wonder about their future careers for good reason. Today, and probably for the next generation, the job market will unquestionably remain turbulent and worrisome. Many have used the hackneyed phrase that career change will take place "in a sea of whitewater." There'll be instability in all economic sectors, not just those that are currently volatile like high technology, investment banking, and telecommunications. With continuing mergers and acquisitions, seemingly capricious layoffs will abound. Companies will continue to be bought and sold on the different stock exchanges, disappearing overnight. And, as experience tells, when firms are acquired or merge, the new conglomerate doesn't necessarily run its business like or even resemble in any way the older independent companies.

New companies will come and go. Dropped from prominence are the hot Internet company Webvan and the highly touted stock analyst favorite, energy trader Enron. Netscape is in a losing battle with Microsoft's Internet Explorer. Google went public in 2004. Once stable utilities, like Pacific Gas and Electric Company (PG&E), MCI World Com, and airline companies such as United, are likely to continue to confront bankruptcy. Consider that Jet Green, the Irish Airline, folded in a week. And half-century-old TWA had to merge with American Airlines. Political and military crises in the Middle East will affect the prices of the fossil fuels and are another "future factor." While Internet companies like Yahoo seem to thrive, keep in mind that its stock price in 2004 was only $27 compared to $230 in 2000. Many investors lost their retirement savings. Jobs in state and local governments will only be as stable as their politically influenced public budgets and voters' willingness to fund new programs will allow. State, county, and city administrators will continue to pray that there won't be a taxpayer revolt.

No job classes, except perhaps positions in homeland, Internet, and computer security, will be immune from horrific loss. After all, it wasn't that long ago that we had keypunch, telex, and phone operators. Companies will continue to experience revolutions in technology, and it's likely that employees will be coached to work more efficiently in order to save time and reduce costs.

Manufacturing positions that are easily automated have been moving overseas in order to increase profits. So have labor intensive service jobs like auditing, accounting, and telemarketing. There's no reason to think that this trend will not continue. While positions have been relocated to Asia, South Asia, and Mexico, countries in Africa may be an outpost for new, automated manufacturing. The only type of work that seems safe from off-shoring is that which requires interfacing with others. So, if people want job protection in their career choice, they should seek positions that require face-to-face communication and also demand some degree of complexity.

What other job characteristics should be considered if job security is important? Quite likely, jobs in the skilled trades may be of greater interest to young people since they can't be sent off shore. Because of our aging population, jobs that cater to older workers and retirees will be increasingly in demand. Degrees in fields like gerontology that specialize in the aging populace may be among those that will provide some security as well.

Even helping service professionals and educators who sacrifice higher salaries for work stability will likely be affected by changes in the future. Consider that counselors are currently losing work while college and university tenure track faculty are being laid off. We have tax cuts and war, the stranglehold of managed care, and the resonating words of Donald Trump saying, "You're fired." New terminology continues to be coined to capture the many changes with words like outsourcing, off-shoring, on-shoring, right-shoring, and a "jobless recovery." Our personal and work lives also include "hyper-tasking," Palm Pilots, Blackberries, Tivo, and DVD burners. Add to all of this the fact that we are in the process of creating a generation of people who seem to have short attention spans coupled with poor eating habits and a lifestyle that is resulting in new and alarming levels of obesity. It's not a pretty picture.

So what does all this turmoil and bad news mean? Newcomers to the job market and people who change jobs will need all the support that they can muster. Everyone's career trail is likely to be bumpy, and everyone will need strong support in deciding upon and managing their career paths. That's why the family is so important. It should be the one place where people can feel safe discussing their ideas and aspirations.

Some Survival Tips

Over the years, every spring I've been asked by the Office of Public Affairs at San Francisco State University to give tips to high school and college graduates as well as job seekers and employment counselors regarding how people should manage their careers, apprenticeships, and college major choices in light of the current economics of the employment markets. Let me offer these sorts of helpful tips for the reader using many of the concepts in earlier chapters. These ideas will demonstrate how the family can be used in an overwhelmingly positive and supportive way in planning for the future.

Mattering

People need to feel that they matter. This has been pointed out on a variety of occasions, but was well articulated by Schlossberg, Lassalle and Golec (1988). Mattering has been defined earlier by Schlossberg,

Lynch, and Chickering (1989) as a perception or belief that people hold onto suggesting that somebody else cares about them, whether that perception is correct or not. And, further, these folks believe that they are the object of that person's attention.

The movie *Cold Mountain,* directed by Anthony Minghella and starring Nicole Kidman, Jude Law, and Renee Zellwiger, surely presents a fine demonstration of the mattering concept. It depicts two would-be lovers who meet briefly and are then separated by civil war for four years. They produce a compendium of letters of love and hope. In spite of the fact that many of their letters never reach their destinations, they both believe not only in their infatuation, but that the other matters greatly to them and appreciates him or her. Based upon the novel by Charles Frazier (1998), the movie demonstrates the power of mattering, even when it exists in an unrealistic fantasy.

People like to be recognized for who they are and for the contributions that they make to others or to the well being of society. And they like to be valued, a feeling that they have when people listen to them and receive their advice and consultation. There is a validation that people experience when they are sought out by others. Mattering has a giving component as well as a receiving component. People matter when they are given advice, and they matter when their advice is listened to.

Amundson (1998) has added to this conceptualization of mattering by suggesting that the more that we help people feel that they matter, the more they may be able to set aside some of their emotional issues when they have to make difficult choices and changes. He believes further that all significant others can be brought in to the process of making career decisions, in part, because they make the people they are involved with feel like they matter.

The advice to people in family relationships is famously simple. Make your family members feel that they count and listen to their ideas, however far flung they may seem to be.

Sam. Sam was 18 and planning for college. He had few vocational interests, but he was passionate about two life enhancing activities, his church youth group and playing his guitar. He certainly wasn't particularly interested in school. College, for the most part, was his parent's idea. They wanted him to be in business, thought that music was akin to paganism and that his alleged interest in church-related work would keep him impoverished for the rest of his life. Interestingly, his parents were quite religious. Fact is, they believed in a strong religion and rigorous education. They just didn't want their children tainting their lives by entering such poorly paid vocations.

Sam received most of his personal sense of mattering and belonging from his friends and didn't feel any career blessings from his parents. He was sure that he, as a person, mattered to them, but his thoughts and ideas about life and career didn't.

Sam had two older sisters who had gone on to pursue their own self-reliant paths. His oldest sister, Ellen, had recently graduated from a small liberal arts college, and she began to take on a role that made Sam feel as if his thoughts about education and career mattered. Since she had just been to college, she knew what services Sam should consider. She told him to stop trying to get information from their parents and instead to consider college campus services that he would find useful. She suggested that when he visited college campuses, he drop into the campus advising center, career services and placement center, and even the counseling center to explore available means of emotional, vocational, and financial support on the campus. Maybe he needed more support than others.

Regarding college major exploration, Ellen advised Sam to not major in a degree program like religion, but rather to explore the many opportunities that the college had to offer. She gave the sisterly advice of taking some classes that he was sure to love and others that he felt he would probably dislike. She thought that it might turn out that he loved the classes he was unsure of and might not be terribly enchanted with the ones he initially thought he would enjoy.

From this talk with Ellen, Sam had gained a different attitude when he finally enrolled in a small religiously oriented college in the Midwest. Sam was able to meet with an advisor who was willing to work with him over the course of his college experience. She opened up a number of doors for Sam, pointing out that perhaps a major in philosophy or history might be useful to pursue as an undergraduate rather than religion which could turn out to be too constricting. She indicated to Sam that there were a variety of job opportunities in the world of religion. These opportunities could be at the local church level and include preaching, religious education, or administration, particularly in larger churches. Furthermore, she noted that there might be career opportunities at the national level that would demand not only graduate work in theology, but could include other advanced degrees in areas as diverse as political science, business administration, or human relations. These could lead to jobs and careers in areas like fundraising, administration, community relations, and relationships with other churches.

Ellen really heard Sam's concerns, and rather than dismissing them, took on a role that made him feel as if he mattered and belonged. His college advisor did the same. Here's a second example.

The Reservationist. I was flying to a meeting in Lancaster, Pennsylvania to give a speech when I was called by the airline company and told that my flight was being cancelled. They directed me to another airline company. Obviously, I was not only taken aback by this predicament but was quite concerned that my trip was about to go awry. My keynote address had been scheduled for over six months.

Of course, I became quite upset with the voice at the other end of the line. But before I became too outrageous, she told me in a deliberate tone that she and 150 of her coworkers at the call center she was housed in were about to be laid off. It was her last day on the job. She was a bit acidic when she told me that, while I had my problems, she had hers.

Instantly, my problems in that moment seemed much less important to me. The counselor in me was touched, and I wanted to assist. In fact, she began to matter to me. And I immediately put on my "career counselor cap." She listened gratefully as I directed her to get the names, business cards, and e-mail addresses from everyone she could at the call center as well as her family. Then, I began to counsel her. I suggested that she write down what she did on the job, going down to the most specific nitty-gritty tasks. Which of these were transferable skills? I asked her to imagine different places or job positions or companies where she could use those skills. Could they be used in selling, or public relations, or database management? I also asked her about her people skills since she had been in contact with people over the phone for years. Finally, I said that she ought to begin to compose a letter, a broadcast letter that she would send out to the people on her e-mail list. There was a pause. Then, in an enthusiastic but teary tone, she told me that I had made her feel very important. She had been devastated by the idea that she would be losing her job. She had felt hopeless and worthless. But, with just a few minutes of my time, she felt that she mattered. She didn't know what she would do for income, and she wasn't sure what she could say to her family. But, she felt that she mattered and that feeling left her, she said, with a sense of her own empowerment.

Before moving on, try to find an image of what mattering means to you. You might be reminded of a friend who has been lost from your life or a person who has passed on. Even a talent that mattered to you could be represented in an image. Then, enumerate 10 people who matter to you as exemplified in the 2 examples. And finally, write down the names of 10 people who you believe that you matter to. At the time of our conversation, that airline reservationist genuinely mattered to me; and I've referred to her in several speeches I've presented. I don't know her name or where she lives, but at some level I believe she sensed that we both mattered to each other.

Don't Make Difficult Decisions Alone

People shouldn't try to manage their problems or make difficult decisions alone. The President of the United States doesn't behave this way, so why should you? Even professional counselors should consult with others on a regular basis to gather an understanding as to how to handle their most difficult clients and to prevent their own occupational burnout. This is reminiscent of a story about a Casey Stengel truism. When Stengel was manager of the New York Yankees in 1958 and was named major league baseball manager of the year, he said something like, "I really don't think I could've won this without those guys on the field."

For many years, I had a personal supervision group that met monthly for dinner. There was a rotating member who paid for the dinner, and the person who had to treat the others was the one who was able to pick the restaurant. Each of us had a "buddy" whom we could call when we felt like we needed some direction or emotional assistance. The experience was a marvelous one for all of us and ended only when one of the members died and others decided to retire from their respective practices. My current practice group at the Career and Personal Development Institute in San Francisco meets regularly for a similar purpose.

Sometimes support can come from extra vocational experiences or hobbies. At an earlier time, I played poker with a number of writers from the *San Francisco Examiner* newspaper. They gathered together to play cards, talk about their stories and mentor other young writers. From this group, I received a lifetime of professional contacts, the chance to hobnob with talented writers, and an opportunity to meet with a group that would listen to my ideas about career development. Because of these connections and the contacts that flowed from them, I've been able to be a part of the print media for many years.

Several years ago, using the precept that people can recover more rapidly from psychological problems if they have assistance from significant others, I wrote *Shared Confinement* (Chope, 2001b). The book sets forth a treatment protocol for agoraphobics that utilizes family members as coaches in the treatment process. I believed that there were methods in which family members could help in the treatment process if they were brought in early by the treating therapist. I thought that there were ways that clients could be given structured support that added to the weekly or twice-weekly interventions of a therapist. Family members could be taught how to coach an agoraphobe, I wrote, through relaxation exercises as well as the many cognitive, behavioral, and cognitive-behavioral treatments that were available. Moreover, they could provide regular and continuous assistance to those who would eventually attempt real life practice by engaging in immersion activities. These could be done more regularly and on a daily basis if a family member could offer support as a coach. So the book was written with this goal in mind. I found that there were ways of assisting the client while also empowering the family member or members who had their lives disrupted by the problem of living with someone who was afraid to go out of the house.

From that book, Andres Consoli and I (Consoli & Chope, 2004) have created a new therapeutic approach that we title Contextual Integrative Psychotherapy (CIP). This approach demonstrates how the utilization of family members in the treatment process can make the therapeutic work more effective and efficient. We believe that, if a family member and client can create a shared world view about a problem along with a working alliance that focuses on an agreement of the goals of treatment and the practice tasks involved, a new, powerful technique can be offered. Fact is, I believe that family can be used quite expeditiously in many forms of psychological counseling.

That is the belief that is offered here as well. Career decisions don't have to be made in a vacuum, and the addition of the support of the family can make the process a more pleasant one using the expertise of interested parties. Extended family members can offer all types of practical advice. In large families, people who have attended different colleges and universities can suggest campuses for relatives considering a college education. In families where a member will be a first generation college student, a wealth of emotional support can be offered. And in looking for work, apprenticeships, volunteering, or part-time projects, family members can be used to generate ideas.

Judith. Judith had her sights set on working in a large law firm in Chicago. She thought she had done reasonably well in law school and the prospect of working in a large firm with the higher salaries and opportunities to be surrounded by the amenities of practice certainly appealed to her. But, throughout the interviewing process, she never was able to obtain the type of position that she expected. She felt like she was beating her head against a wall as she pursued opportunities unsuccessfully. Jobs even in smaller firms and in lesser known public service positions seemed to be unavailable to her.

The reasons given were many. She hadn't attended a topflight law school, and she was in approximately the middle of her class when she began to apply for work. But no strategy seemed to accomplish what she hoped for. She was discussing her predicament at a family gathering when her uncle, who was a college professor, suggested that perhaps she might consider work in a university, something she had never considered.

He said that she could work in the general counsel's office as one possibility, but she could also work in the grants office doing contract approvals or the affirmative action office ensuring compliance with Federal regulations. He also indicated that she might want to think of working for the faculty labor union as a negotiator.

While these ideas were clearly outside what Judith had thought would be her career path, the advice inculcated a feeling of hope and a belief that she would be able to find some work in law that would prove to be exciting along with a reasonable salary. No one besides her uncle had recommended that she consider this type of work in the law. It was his input, not her own professional network that led to hope and enthusiasm for her.

I don't want to romanticize the point that the impact of family networks will always produce creative ideas for one's career pursuits; but trying to come up with alternative career plans by yourself, when your "Plan A" goes awry, is terribly inefficient. Attention should be focused upon the need to foster relationships, and the family can be an important part of a network that can support you and keep your career decision making from a solo flight into disarray.

Build and Maintain a Strong Network

Everyone needs to establish and maintain a strong network. Individual connections are a job seeker's most important asset. But this turns out to be a task that is, perhaps, more difficult than it seems on its face. In Robert Putnam's *Bowling Alone* (2000), the argument is made that American society for years has been losing its social capital, connections with each other and community. Putnam believes that this can lead to a bankruptcy in our sense of community and belongingness. Americans, according to data from surveys he cites, belong to fewer civic organizations, vote less frequently and hardly know their neighbors. Putnam is convincing in his insinuation that the changes in how we work-often alone in a cubicle, relax at home with television, computers and electronic games, and experience the new roles of women as individual breadwinners have created an atmosphere of going alone. These changes lend credence to the thesis he promulgates that the most fundamental form of social capital is the family. And there is certainly compelling data that indicate that the bonds of the nuclear and extended family may be weakening for many of the reasons described in the book.

So why is this a problem for the job seeker? Well, the evidence has been in for almost twenty years. In the high technology age with the many swanky Web sites, employment obtained over the Internet accounts for approximately 4% of all hires: personal and professional contacts account for over 50% (Bolles, 2001). Most people get their jobs by who they know. And the people that we seem to know first and foremost don't come from many of the formal settings that we find ourselves in; they are our family. So, in any job search, people need an up-to-date e-mail address book, beginning with the immediate as well as the extended family. People can use holiday card lists to begin the process. I had the airline reservationist create an e-mail list of family members and colleagues on the day that she was being let go.

Everyone ought to consider creating an e-mail list of their family members to stay in touch and to receive support in times of need. Most job hunters and career decision makers forget to consider this simple task. But with mobility of family members around the country and the world, it isn't many degrees of separation before it's possible to find a family member in a distant area. That person can help to develop ideas and promote opportunities and might provide a place to stay if there is a need to search for work in a different part of the country.

In addition to keeping the e-mail contacts, people can let everyone in their family address book know what kind of work they are looking for by sending out a broadcast letter informing the family members of exactly what kind of opportunities they are looking for. They can ask family members in the broadcast letters to suggest possibilities that may be in their area, and they can elicit suggestions for new ways to use their skill set. Activities like these can help a job seeker to be focused and direct with clear objectives honed by concerned family members. If someone is unable to name what he or she is searching for, then selected relatives in the network can be used to generate ideas or point to new possibilities. Most important, people need to stay plugged in even when they aren't looking for work.

Not only do I use my family to stay plugged in, but I use my larger extended family of graduates from the Career Counseling Program in the Counseling Department at San Francisco State University. Some of my students have gone on to become established writers, adding to their own workplace eminence. Al Levin who graduated in the mid-1980s is the coauthor of *Luck is No Accident* (Krumboltz & Levin, 2004). The book advocates the consideration of luck and happenstance in the career decision making process. Susan Maltz, another graduate of the program, wrote a book with several others titled *A Fork in the Road.* It's about career choice for teens (Maltz, Grahn, & Vega, 2003). And Carol Gelatt, who was a student early in my career, writes regularly with her husband H. B. Gelatt (Gelatt & Gelatt, 2003).

Louis. The best example of how family members can help a career path may be in a situation experienced by my 15-year-old nephew, Louis. Louis has had two bands. The first was "Supermonkeys" and, in that band he was a drummer and vocalist. His new band is "Odd Man Out," and he is now a guitarist and vocalist. The boys in the band write all of their own music and have won many contests in South Florida's continuing Battle of the Bands. But they received their greatest opportunity because of their network and a little bit of the serendipitous luck that Krumboltz and Levin (2004) refer to.

Bruce Springsteen has a daughter in Florida who participates in the Palm Beach Area Winter Equestrian Festival. Springsteen also works out in a fitness center when he is visiting to watch his daughter participate in the festival. Turns out that the mother of the "Odd Man Out" drummer is a trainer at the facility where Springsteen exercises. The mother persistently invited Springsteen to come to hear her son play in his band, indicating that the band was receiving terrific reviews and had even been invited to play at CBGBs in Greenwich Village in New York City, the club where the Ramones got their start. Finally, Springsteen showed up at a concert, listened to the music and later had his picture taken with the band. This was all nicely documented in an article by Palm Beach Post writer Leslie Gray Streeter (2004). Apparently, Springsteen's daughter, along with several thousand other early teenage girls, loves the band. Since meeting Springsteen, the boys have been able to open for Cindy Lauper in a concert in Florida and have performed at CBGBs. After their performance in New York, they received wonderful reviews in the *Village Voice,* which helped them to win a spot on the "Regis and Kelly" television program. All this occurred as a result of musical talent, a mother's connection, and happenstance.

Know Your Talents

Everyone reading this book has accrued both specific and transferable skills. You should know what these are and keep track of them. Everyone should practice selling these to family as well as to friends. Resumés and cover letters should be crafted so that these attributes sparkle. Ensure that key words employers use for their job postings appear on the resumé along with a clear job objective. This is an arena where the family can be quite useful both as a source of support and a gentle critic.

Know your talents surely goes without saying. But you should also know how to sell them. Many of you have not only earned a degree or have a professional license, but have accrued both specific and transferable skills. Know what these are and keep track of them. Practice selling these to friends and family who'll listen. Counselors can be assisted in marketing their skills with the free copy of "Public Awareness Ideas and Strategies for Professional Counselors" from the American Counseling Association. Be specific about what you know. Use family members, even younger siblings, to keep you on track.

You might even try this exercise. When practicing the selling of ideas or talents, act as if the practice is being performed in front of a fifth-grader. When you can explain difficult concepts to a younger person, it forces clarity. It also forces excitement to keep this younger person from becoming bored.

I specialize in two areas: career counseling and anxiety disorders. I wrote *Dancing Naked* (Chope, 2000) to integrate career and personal issues, a passion of mine. Many people have asked why I titled the book *Dancing Naked*. When I was a little boy, I watched John Wayne movies. As the good guy, he would shoot his pistol at the feet of the bad guys with the line, "I'm gonna make you dance." And I thought that having your feet shot at reminded me of a job interview with one aspect missing. In the job interview, you also feel so vulnerable it's like you don't have many clothes on. Family members who are in your corner can make you feel less vulnerable.

Family members can spend some time generating ideas about self-promotion. They can also review resumés and cover letters and lend suggestions for improvement.

It is often difficult for people to receive information that they can trust. Even Putnam (2000) pointed out that Americans appear to be less trusting. Between 1960 and 1993, the proportion of people who said that most people can be trusted fell by 58%. He adds that the overall decrease in social trust is even higher when education is controlled for. So people have a tendency to not trust and, in doing so, are often wary of putting themselves out to others to explore their assets and deficits and find ways in which their method of marketing themselves can improve.

When people have asked me what is the most efficient way of getting an evaluation of their skills, talents, resumés, cover letters, and so forth, I've suggested that they begin with having a party, perhaps even a family party. There can be a gathering where one or two people who are considering college or career decisions can be the focus of attention and receive help and suggestions from family members. There is strength and creativity in this type of experience.

With the current technological innovations, there is a subtle pressure for people to engage in this exploratory process alone. After all, you sit at the computer alone, searching for information alone, composing alone while peering at your screen. Countless Web sites provide opportunities to evaluate skills and interests and values. But doing self-assessment in the home may not be right for the vast majority of people. After finding out what skills one has from engaging in an online evaluation, you may not know what to do with the information. Even the government Web site O*Net has terrific brief testing of abilities, interests, and occupational needs. And, after a person completes the instruments, he or she also receives input on the types of jobs available for people with these profiles. But this is a lot of data to digest, and it may be only the beginning of what a person needs. Generally, people in this situation need some interaction with others. That's where the family can help.

I've had the occasion of working with many clients who received the information I've described from different Web sites and then didn't know what to do with the information. For many, it is useful to see a professional career counselor to help with making meaning out of information that is obtained from skills testing. But the generation of ideas as to where a person might use talents can come from well meaning family members. Family members can suggest creative alternatives.

Consider Relocating

We live in a highly mobile society and among a highly mobile workforce. Part of the difficulty that people have with the workforce is what Putnam (2000) has referred to as the "repotting hypothesis." Frequent mobility and "repotting" tends to disrupt root systems. But family support can help. Family contact can make you feel less uprooted, freeing you to pursue positions that may be out of the area. And you might get lucky. Sometimes, even if a company says they're hiring in Los Angeles, they may have a similar position right at home. But you'd never know that if you didn't send a resumé to the company in Los Angeles.

A geographic challenge becomes another arena where family members in other parts of the country can help. Amundson and Borgen (1987) pointed out that one of the greatest dangers in the career decision making process is in the isolation. This is doubly true for those who are going to relocate. Gathering assistance from family members who have lived in particular locations or states can provide useful information about cost of housing, taxes, economic prospects, and the like.

Aaron. Aaron wanted to move to Las Vegas to work in the hotel and event planning business. As his counselor, I was concerned that moving to this area would result in loneliness and depression. He was leaving his home and close family ties and moving into a place of relative unknown. I had images of him living in a small studio apartment becoming isolated from others as he found it increasingly difficult to look for work in his area of interest.

I thought that it would be useful for him to connect to a religious community as he had been very involved in a parish in his home town. But I also wanted him to begin to search for relatives in his extended family who might have worked in the area at one time or had experience in the hotel industry and could serve as a sounding board for him.

With that plan, Aaron was able to make the e-mail list of extended family contacts and located a cousin who had worked in Nevada. His cousin was able to offer Aaron advice on where to live, what clubs to attend, and where the best bargains were for furniture and accessories. This insider information plus church membership did the trick. With this help, Aaron was able to get beyond the potential loneliness that he feared.

Consider a Portfolio Job Search

Instead of seeking full-time employment, you might want to try several part-time positions for a while. That will build your talent base and add to your growing network of contacts. Artists, actresses, and actors have used this approach for years. Acting is always part-time work, so many of the individuals in this profession need to supplement their income when they aren't on stage. So, the family can foster instrumental support by generating these types of ideas as well.

One of our program graduates is Velina Brown, an actress with the American Conservatory Theater in San Francisco as well as with the San Francisco Mime Troop. After watching her perform one evening in San Francisco at the A.C.T., I decided to go to meet her in the Green Room of the Geary Theater to chide her about not utilizing her Master's degree in career counseling. With a wily smile, she queried, "Dr. Chope, what makes you think I'm not using my career counseling degree?" With that, she pulled out a brochure from her backpack and gave it to me. The brochure described her career counseling practice, and it was titled "Career Counseling for Actors and Actresses." She pointed out that since stage actors like her are always looking for their next gig, they need help in finding part-time employment that is consistent with their education and training. Accordingly, I have sometimes referred to this concept as the "Actor/Actress Model of Career Decision Making." It is indicative of the job searches of people engaged in project driven work situations.

It is quite common in the current economy to create multiple income streams. I characterize my own career as one made up of different income streams. For example, I teach, write, speak, consult, counsel, coach, and do stand up comedy routines. These income streams can fluctuate. The only income I can count on is that from my job as a university professor. The comedy club routine has never made a bean, but is still fun.

But there are other reasons for considering more than one income stream. Our economy is moving into an area of project-driven employment. Many people are now hired for a project, not for a job, lifetime, or career. What is most important in this respect is for people to continue to work, develop new skills, and create a larger network.

As part of this consideration, I think it's useful to consider aiming lower in the job search. We are also witnessing an area of matrix organizational charting, not linear charting. You can begin again at the bottom, but you may move laterally and then up. So it's conceivable that one of the part-time jobs that you obtain will be at a level below what you had expected. But it is possible with many organizations to move laterally and then move up in a zigzag rather than a more linear process.

Be a Walk-On

If you believe that you have talent to add to the intellectual capital of an organization, then ask for a tryout. Offer to take on a short term project that you'll deliver, without cost, to demonstrate your knowledge base. Some professional and college athletes do this and the model works in a market where employers need help but don't advertise positions. Be a volunteer walk-on and try to get some ideas for these opportunities from your family. Billionaire Warren Buffet of Berkshire Hathaway has famously suggested this when he said, "Decide who you want to work for and pursue that work, even if you volunteer for a while." I call this the "Walk-On Athlete Model of Career Decision Making." I've had terrific success with this model.

Jennifer. I had worked with Jennifer for several months as she pursued a career in sound engineering and editing. She wanted to work for a local broadcasting facility or in one of the major film studios in the San Francisco Bay Area, like Pixar, Zoetrope, Lucasfilm, or Fantasy Studios. She had tried everything to get in. Her family was in the area, and she had developed contacts through them as well as the career center at a local college and the network of colleagues she had created in previous work and internships in film. She was going to take another part-time position when I suggested she volunteer at one of the film studios for a day or two a week. This would be like an internship or apprenticeship. She needed to cognitively fashion the idea so that she didn't feel that her time and expertise was being totally ripped off. Her mother had an old friend who was an executive at one of the studios, and, while Jennifer had called this person to secure employment, he had nothing to offer her. But she called him again with the intention of volunteering in the sound editing facility at the studio. He put her in touch with the head of sound editing and she was able to volunteer two days a week

While this approach had originally seemed to be a good idea, it started to unravel when Jennifer wasn't able to segue into full-time work. She had been volunteering for two months and was close to throwing in the towel. But, while on a weekend camping trip, she was contacted by the studio to come back home right away as they needed her expertise. A staffer had quit suddenly, and she was the only other person with experience on the project who could keep it on schedule. At that moment, despite being filled with glee, she was able to ask about a contract and regular full-time work on the project through its completion. She secured that, demonstrating that being a "walk-on" could indeed create a positive occupational experience. It would not have happened without her mother's assistance.

Regularly Review Your Decisions

Too often, we think of our career decisions as, in some ways, final. Yet they should really be considered transient and subject to periodic review. The Gelatts (2003) have suggested that you need to be focused and flexible in what you do and to treat your goals as hypotheses. To me, this suggests a never ending type of decision making model. People describe this in different ways, like managing your career mobility or ensuring that you're aware of the choices that you have available to you. People are often able to manage their career decisions by knowing which opportunities seem to be the best for them. This usually involves moving into new positions that provide new skill opportunities along with the chance to increase earning power.

And, in a similar vein, it is important to use your imagination. I mentioned in *Dancing Naked* that Einstein thought that his greatest contribution to the world was his imagination, not his intelligence or his knowledge of astrophysics. He was able to engage in a balancing of information with imagination, a task that the Gelatts suggest as well. Interestingly, Einstein, because of his manner of creative thinking and use of imagination, was asked to be the first Prime Minister of the new state of Israel. Of course, he turned it down. He said that it wouldn't add to his knowledge or interest in science and would be too time consuming.

In the 21st century, creativity is demanded from everyone. And families can help here, too. Creative questioning is becoming a part of the job search process. Human resources professionals now recommend that job seekers read books like *How Would You Move Mt. Fuji?* (Poundstone, 2003). To evaluate creative thinking and imagination, interviewers are asking questions that seem to resemble brain teasers. Several companies have used the following teaser. Try this for yourself.

You drive past three people on a corner in your hot two-seater: a very sick old man, a lost love of your life, and your best friend who once saved you during a terrible accident. Who do you pick up? Human Resources professionals at companies like IBM say about one in twenty get the creative, imaginative answer they are seeking. That answer is to get out of the car, ask your friend to get in and drive the sick old man to the hospital, while you wait at the bus stop with the love of your life, hopefully getting a chance to re-engage. The question reflects a new attitude toward employees and what companies seek. Hiring committees want people who can stand on their own and quickly give creative solutions to curious problems.

Creative evaluation has become a new marketplace. I have a friend from college who was part of a start-up company called the Big Idea Group. Their goal was to solicit ideas from developers of products like toys, games, and other instruments, select a few of these to sponsor, and then create the manufacturing, marketing, advertising, and distribution plan for the product. They were looking for what has been called "the next big thing," although theirs was limited to toys and games. Families can help here as well with "out of the box" questioning.

By regularly reviewing your decisions and maintaining your creativity while stimulating your imagination, you'll prepare yourself for a world that demands an enlightened way of looking at things. Regularly review information on the Internet regarding changes in your profession along with new opportunities. This probably sounds like you won't be loyal to a company. But, frankly, company loyalty has really gone the way of moats and drawbridges.

Go ahead and post a resumé at a site if you wish. But don't expect miracles. Job searching is hard work. Still, help is on the way. Today there are even Web sites for people to increase the size of their network, like www.ryze.com and www.linkedin.com.

Become a Student of the Instability Around You

The last idea takes us full circle from the beginning of the chapter and the book. Your opportunities will come from the instability of the workplace. A supportive family will help to center you in these uncertain times. While there are disasters like Enron and MCI World Com, there will emerge new companies with new ways of doing business. New mergers and acquisitions will create new opportunities for teambuilding.

The war in Iraq and the aftermath will create new opportunities and responsibilities for counselors to serve the public. Returning veterans will be in need of transitioning services, and more than a few will change careers. Others will need new skills training as their former jobs morph into something that hardly resembles what they left behind.

The use of computers with online chat, coaching, and training on "Blackboard" will change how people are taught. Distance learning will become commonplace. Many of you undoubtedly have your own Web site, weblog, or a webmaster who can coach and train you either in your home or over the Internet. Traditional college professors are becoming an anachronism.

There will be new opportunities in the growing field of social entrepreneurship as more people become interested in activities where they can do work that they believe benefits society while they are also able to generate a profit. People can express their family core values in new and exciting ways. The magazine *Fast Company* (2004), along with assistance from the Monitor group, a global consulting firm, evaluates entrepreneurship and publicizes the best of these efforts not just for their social good, but rather for their prominence as entrepreneurial endeavors. Their evaluative criteria illustrate how you could evaluate yourself or a particular job you may be interested in. The best programs:

> Focus on entrepreneurship: They can gather appropriate resources.
>
> Are innovative: They engage in creative renewal and form partnerships with organizations that already are able to function with venture capital.
>
> Have a social impact: They make a difference.
>
> Are ambitious: They want the employees to stretch themselves.
>
> Are sustainable: They can generate the resources to keep on growing.

The Rubicon Programs in Richmond, California, are one of these unique social entrepreneurship programs. They offer two trades, baking and landscape services. But they only employ homeless, mentally challenged, or substance addicted workers. The executive director of the program is Rick Aubry, a psychoanalytically trained psychologist who quit his clinical practice to be part of a new enterprise that was going to help to change the world. The program is certainly an inspiration for those in need, but it is also an inspiration for those who want to enter the business world, earn a good wage, and do something that is socially worthwhile. These positions may be the new waves of the future.

The workforce is changing in other ways. We have new acronyms for over-stretched workers in two-career families: "DINS" (dual income no sex) or "DINK" (dual income no kids). Women are now 47% of the workforce and get 57% of the degrees and in 30% of the households earn more than their husbands. Eighty-seven percent of the households with two adults have two workers. Less than 30% of the U.S. population is under 18. If the low birthrate continues, we may actually run out of workers. The largest generation in history is 60% of the workforce. The cohorts to follow may be too small to maintain the current workload.

Career counselors ought to focus more of their efforts on the disenfranchised. For example, over two million people are in prison. Sixty-seven percent of those in prison had not worked before being incarcerated. Thirty-five percent of inner city youth are not only unemployed, they do not look for work. And most of our programs for the long-term unemployed have not been successful. Career counselors will need to step up to the plate and develop more creative programming for these groups.

Maintain Your Vision, Flexibility, and Adaptability Along with Realistic Expectations

Maybe this is where the family can help the most. The Gelatts warn people to be focused and flexible. The difficult decisions that we all make take us on a journey. Sometimes it takes us where we want to go and other times we end up somewhere else. Ironically, the somewhere else may be the best place for us to be.

Chapter Summary

This chapter has presented the challenges for the future. It has offered many ideas that families can use to help job seekers in appropriate and powerful ways. Most importantly, the family can improve the individual self-esteem of the members by making them feel that they matter. They can offer evaluative assistance and provide well-placed contacts from their own network. While the world of work will continue to be in some turmoil, family members can support job seekers when they try innovative approaches to securing work, like being a walk-on or creating a portfolio career. The growing field of social entrepreneurship may have some of the most exciting opportunities for the future and may also be a method to mobilize the long-term unemployed.

References

Alderfer, C. (2004). A family therapist's reaction to "The influences of the family of origin on career development: A review and analysis." *The Counseling Psychologist, 32,* 569-577.

American Psychological Association (2002). John D. Krumboltz: Award for distinguished professional contributions to knowledge. *American Psychologist, 57,* 928-931.

Amundson, N. E. (1998*). Active engagement: Enhancing the career counseling process.* Richmond, B.C., Canada: Ergon Communications.

Amundson, N. E., & Borgen, W. A. (1987). Coping with unemployment: What helps and hinders. *Journal of Employment Counseling, 24,* 97-106.

Aron, W. (2003, August 25). Every Jewish mother's worst nightmare. *Newsweek,* 14.

Australian Broadcasting Company (ABC). (June 16, 2003). Enough rope with Andrew Denton: Interview with Jim Carrey [transcript from television series episode]. Retrieved April 19, 2005, from http://www.abc.net.au.enoughrope/stories/s880946.htm.

Bandura, A. (1977). Self efficacy: Toward a unifying theory of behavioral change. *Psychological Review, 84,* 191-251.

Barber, J. (1992). *The presidential character.* Upper Saddle River, NJ: Prentice Hall.

Benson, H. (2004, June 6). The latest author angry at Bush, Joseph Wilson has deep roots in S.F. *The San Francisco Chronicle,* pp. E1, E4.

Blustein, D. (1995). Toward a contextual perspective of the school-to-work transition: A reaction to Feij et al. *Journal of Vocational Behavior, 46,* 257-265.

Blustein, D., Fama, L., White, S., Ketterson, T., Schaefer, B., Schwam, M., Sirin, S., & Skau, M. (2001). A qualitative analysis of counseling case material: Listening to our clients. *The Counseling Psychologist, 29,* 240-258.

Blustein, D., Phillips, S., Jobin-Davis, K., Finkelberg, S., & Roarke, A. (1997). A theory-building investigation of the school-to-work transition. *The Counseling Psychologist, 25*, 364-402.

Blustein, D. L. (1992). Applying current theory and research in career exploration to practice. *Career Development Quarterly, 41*, 171-184.

Blustein, D. L. (1997). A context-rich perspective of career exploration across the life span. *Career Development Quarterly, 45*, 3, 260-264.

Blustein, D. L. (2001). The interface of work and relationships: Critical knowledge for 21st century psychology. *The Counseling Psychologist, 29*, 179-192.

Blustein, D. L., Walbridge, M. M., Friedlander, M. L., & Palladino, D. E. (1991). Contributions of psychological separation and parental attachment to the career development process. *Journal of Counseling Psychology, 38*, 39-50.

Bodley, H. (2004, July 22). On Baseball: Eckersley looks to help save others. *USA Today*. Retrieved April 19, 2005, from http://www.usatoday.com.

Bolles, R. N. (2001). *What color is your parachute?* Berkeley, CA: Ten Speed Press.

Bordin, E. S. (1979). The generalizability of the working alliance. *Psychotherapy: Theory, Research and Practice, 16*, 252-260.

Bowen, M. (1978). *Family therapy in clinical practice*. New York: Jason Aronson.

Bowlby, J. (1982). *Attachment and loss: Vol. 1. Attachment* (2nd ed.). New York: Basic Books.

Bratcher, W. E. (1982). The influence of the family on career selection: A family system's perspective. *Personnel and Guidance Journal, 61*, 87-91.

Bridges, W. (1995). *Jobshift: How to prosper in a workplace without jobs*. New York: Addison-Wesley.

Brown, M. (2004). The career development influence of family of origin: Considerations of race/ethnic group membership and class. *The Counseling Psychologist, 32*, 587-595.

CACREP. (2001). *2001 Standards*. Alexandria, VA: CACREP. Retrieved May 19, 2004, from http://www.cacrep.org/2001Standards.html.

Chartrand, J. M., Robbins, S.,& Morrill, W. (2002). *Career factors inventory (A)*. Palo Alto, CA: Consulting Psychologists Press.

Chope, R., & Fang, F. (1999). Career counseling for new Chinese immigrants: Clinical issues and practical recommendations. *College of Education Review, 10*, 54-59.

Chope, R. C. (2000). *Dancing naked: Breaking through the emotional limits that keep you from the job you want*. Oakland, CA: New Harbinger Publications.

Chope, R. C. (2001a). Influence of the family in career decision making: Identity development, career path and life planning. *Career Planning and Adult Development Journal, 17*, 54-64.

Chope, R. C. (2001b). *Shared confinement: Healing options for you and the agoraphobic in your life*. Oakland, CA: New Harbinger Publications.

Chope, R. C. (2002). *Family matters: Influences of the family in career decision making*. Greensboro, NC: ERIC Counseling & Students Services Clearinghouse. (ERIC Document Reproduction Service No. ED470005)

Chope, R. C. (2003). Using the family of origin in career counseling. In G. Walz & R. Knowdell (Eds.), *Global realities: Celebrating our differences, honoring our connections*. Greensboro, NC: CAPS Press.

Cochran, L. (1997). *Career counseling: A narrative approach*. Thousand Oaks: Sage.

Consoli, A. J., & Chope, R. C. (2005). Contextual integrative psychotherapy: A case study. In G. Stricker & J. Gold (Eds.), *A casebook of psychotherapy integration*. Washington, DC: American Psychological Association.

Dagley, J. (1984*). A vocational genogram*. Athens, GA: University of Georgia.

Dawis, R. V., & Lofquist, L. H. (1984). *A psychological theory of work adjustment*. Minneapolis, MN: University of Minnesota Press.

deVries, B., Birren, J., & Deutchman, D. (1990). Adult development through guided autobiography: The family context. *Family Relations, 39*, 3-7.

deVries, B., Birren, J., & Deutchman, D. (1995). Method and uses of the guided autobiography. In B. Haight & J. Webster (Eds.), *The Art and Science of Reminiscing: Theory, Research, Methods, and Applications*. New York: Taylor & Francis.

Dorgu, S. (1994). Determinants of parental involvement in a support program: A study of communication behavior and information sources (Doctoral dissertation, Syracuse University, 1993). *Dissertation Abstracts International, 54*, 2796.

Eigen, C. A., Hartman, B. W., & Hartman, P. T. (1987). Relations between family interaction patterns and career indecision. *Psychological Reports, 60*, 87-94.

Flores, L., & Heppner, M. (2002). Multicultural career counseling: Ten essentials for training. *Journal of Career Development, 28*, 181-190.

Fast Company (2004). *The change masters: Social capitalist project explained*. Retrieved February 25, 2005, from www.fastcompany.com/social/2005/explanation.

Frazier, C. (1998). *Cold mountain*. New York: Vintage.

Gans, C. (2004, July 10). Celebrating 50 years of Jazz at Newport. *San Francisco Chronicle,* pp. E6.

Gelatt, H. B. (1989). Positive uncertainty: A new decision making framework for counseling. *Journal of Counseling Psychology, 36*, 252-256.

Gelatt, H. B., & Gelatt, C. (2003). *Creative decision making using positive uncertainty*. Menlo Park, CA: Crisp Publications.

Gelardin, S. (Ed.). (2001). Family influences on career choice and success [Special issue]. *Career Planning and Adult Development Journal, 17.*

Gladding, S. T. (1995). *Group work: A counseling speciality* (2nd ed.). Englewood Cliffs, NJ: Prentice Hall

Gottfredson, G. D., & Holland, J. L. (1989). *Dictionary of Holland Occupational Codes* (2nd ed.). Odessa, FL: Psychological Assessment Resources.

Gysbers, N.C., Heppner, M. J., & Johnston, J. A. (2003). *Career counseling: Process, issues, and techniques* (2nd ed.). Boston: Allyn and Bacon.

Gysbers, N. C., & Moore, E. J. (1973). *Life career development: A model.* Columbia, MO: University of Missouri.

Hackett, G., & Betz, N. (1981). A self efficacy approach to the career development of women. *Journal of Vocational Behavior, 18,* 326-29.

Harris, J. (1998). *The nurture assumption: Why children turn out the way they do.* New York: The Free Press.

Hartung, P. J., Lewis, D. M., May, K., & Niles, S. G. (2000). Family interaction patterns and career development. Paper presented at the 108th annual meeting of the American Psychological Association, Washington, DC.

Hayley, J. (1991). *Problem solving therapy* (2nd ed). San Francisco: Jossey-Bass.

Helms, J. (1995). An update of Helm's white and people of color racial identity models. In J. Ponterotto, J. Casas, L. Suzuki, & C. Alexander (Eds.), *Handbook of multicultural counseling* (pp. 181-198). Thousand Oaks, CA: Sage.

Hendricks, T. (2003, August 10). Literacy legacy sold in Oakland. *San Francisco Chronicle*, p. A15.

Herr, E. L., & Lear, P. B. (1984). The family as an influence on career development. *Family Therapy Collections, 10,* 1-15.

Holland, J. L. (1985). Making vocational choices: A theory of personalities and work environments (2nd ed.). Englewood Cliffs, NJ: Prentice-Hall.

Jacobsen, M. H. (2000). *Hand-me-down dreams: How families influence our career paths*. New York: Three Rivers Press.

Jenkins, L. (2004, June 13). Peterson blends Met's pitching staff with science and an artist's touch. *The New York Times*, pp. D1, D3.

Johnson, B. D., Thompson, J. M., McCrudden, C., & Franklin, L. C. (1998). Relation between attachment style and Holland's personality types. Paper presented at the 106th annual meeting of the American Psychological Association, San Francisco, CA.

Kaplan, D. M. (2003). *Family counseling for all counselors*. Greensboro, NC: CAPS Publications.

Kelly, G. A. (1955). *A theory of personality: The psychology of personal constructs*. New York: Norton.

Kenny, M. E., & Donaldson, G. (1992). The relationship of parental attachment and psychological separation to the adjustment of first year college women. *Journal of College Student Development, 33,* 431-438.

Kim, B., Atkinson, D., & Umemoto, D. (2001). Asian cultural values and the counseling process: Current knowledge and directions for future research. *The Counseling Psychologist, 29,* 570-603.

Kinnier, R. T., Brigman, S. L., & Noble, F. C. (1990). Career indecision and family enmeshment. *Journal of Counseling and Development, 68,* 309-312.

Krents, H. (1972). *To race the wind.* New York: Putnam

Krumboltz, J. D. & Levin, A. S. (2004*). Luck is no accident.* Atascadero, CA: Impact Publishers.

Kuehl, B. (1995). The solution-oriented genogram: A collaborative approach. *Journal of Marriage and the Family, 21,* 239-250.

Lee, E. (1983). Assessment and treatment of Chinese immigrant families. *Journal of Psychotherapy and the Family, 6,* 99-122.

Lerner, M. E. (2000, September 29/October 1). Facing your fear. *USA Weekend*, pp. 8-11.

Lopez, F. G. (1989). Current family dynamics, trait anxiety, and academic adjustment: Test of a family-based model of vocational identity. *Journal of Vocational Behavior, 35*, 76-87.

Luft, J., & Ingham, H. (1955). The Johari window, a graphic model of interpersonal awareness. *Proceedings of the Western Training Laboratory in Group Development.* Los Angeles: UCLA Extension Office.

Maltz, S., Grahn, B., & Vega, J. (2003). *A fork in the road: A career planning guide for young adults.* Atascadero, CA: Impact Publishers.

McCormick, R. M., & Amundson, N. E. (1997). A career-life planning model for First Nations people. *Journal of Employment Counseling. 34*, 171-179.

McDaniels, C., & Gysbers, N. C. (1992). *Counseling for career development: Theories, resources, and practice.* San Francisco: Jossey-Bass.

Minuchin, S. (1974). *Families and family therapy.* Cambridge, MA: Harvard University Press.

Mitchell, K. E., Levin, A. S., & Krumboltz, J. D. (1999). Planned happenstance: Constructing unexpected career opportunities. *Journal of Counseling and Development, 77*, 115-124.

Mitchell, L. K., & Krumboltz, J. D. (1990). Social learning approach to career decisionmaking: Krumboltz's theory. In D. Brown, L. Brooks, & Associates, Career choice and development: Applying contemporary theories to practice (2nd. ed., pp. 308-337). San Francisco: Jossey-Bass.

Moos, R. H. (1986). *Work environment scale* (2nd ed.). Palo Alto, CA: Consulting Psychologists Press.

Moos, R. H., & Moos, B. S. (1981). *Family environment scale.* Palo Alto, CA: Consulting Psychologists Press.

Nakao, A. (2004, March 7). Firing line: The accidental hero. *The San Francisco Chronicle*, pp.E7, E12.

National Career Development Association. (1997). *Career counseling competencies*. Tulsa, OK: National Career Development Association.

National Career Development Association Professional Standards Committee. (1997). *Career counseling competencies*. Alexandria, VA: National Career Development Association.

Niles, S. G., & Harris-Bowlsbey, J. (2002). *Career development interventions in the 21st century*. Upper Saddle River, NJ: Merrill Prentice Hall.

Nolte, C. (2004, June 13). Charles W. Dullea - Changed USF as president in the '60s. *San Francisco Chronicle*, p. B7.

Okiishi, R. W. (1987). The genogram as a tool in career counseling. *Journal of Counseling and Development, 66*, 139-143.

Papp, P., & Imber-Black, E. (1996). Family themes: Transmission and transformation. *Family Process, 35*, 5-20.

Parsons, F. (1909). *Choosing a vocation*. Boston: Houghton Mifflin.

Penick, N. I., & Jepson, D. A. (1992). Family functioning and adolescent career development. *Career Development Quarterly, 40*, 208-222.

Peterson, N., & Gonzalez, R. (2005). The role of work in people's lives: Applied career counseling and vocational psychology (2nd ed.). Pacific Grove, CA: Brooks Cole.

Phillips, S. S., Christopher-Sisk, E. K., & Gravino, K. L. (2001). Making career decisions in a relational context. *The Counseling Psychologist, 29*, 193-213.

Pika, J., Maltese, J., & Thomas, N. (2002). *The politics of the presidency*. Washington, DC: CQ Press.

Pope, M. (2000). A brief history of career counseling in the United States. *Career Development Quarterly, 48*, 194-211.

Poundstone, W. (2003). *How would you move Mt. Fuji? Microsoft's cult of the puzzle-How the world's smartest company selects the most creative thinkers.* Boston: Little Brown & Co.

Public Broadasting System (PBS). *American experience, people and events: Billy Carter 1937-1988.* Retrieved April 19, 2005, from http://www.pbs.org [Search for Billy Carter].

Putnam, R. D. (2000). *Bowling alone.* New York: Simon and Schuster.

Remen, R. N. (1996). *Kitchen table wisdom.* New York: Putnam.

Rifkin, J. (1995). *The end of work.* New York: Putnam.

Roe, A. (1957). Early determinants of career choice. *Journal of Counseling Psychology, 4,* 212-217.

Russert, T. (2004). *Big Russ and me.* New York: Random House.

Satir, V. (1983). *Conjoint family therapy* (3rd ed.). Palo Alto, CA: Science and Behavior Books.

Satir, V. (1988). *The new people making.* Palo Alto, CA: Science and Behavior Books.

Satir, V., & Baldwin, M. (1983). *Satir step by step.* Palo Alto, CA: Science and Behavior Books.

Savickas, M. (1995). Constructivist counseling for career indecision. *Career Development Quarterly, 43,* 363-373.

Schevitz, T. (2002, September 26). Surprise on poll of Cal students. *San Francisco Chronicle,* p. A27.

Schlossberg, N. K., Lassalle, A., & Golec, R. (1988). *The mattering scale for adults in higher education* (6th ed.). College Park, MD: University of Maryland.

Schlossberg, N. K., Lynch, A. Q., & Chickering, A. W. (1989). *Improving higher education environments for adults.* San Francisco, CA :Jossey-Bass.

Schulenberg, J. E., Vondracek, F., & Crouter, A. (1984). The influence of the family on vocational development. *Journal of Marriage and the Family, 46*, 129-143.

Schultheiss, D., Kress, H., Manzi, A., & Glasscock, J. (2001). Relational influences in career development: A qualitative inquiry. *The Counseling Psychologist, 29*, 214-239.

Shea, J. (2004, June 6). Degree of difficulty: Draft system makes college grads rare in MLB. *The San Francisco Chronicle*, p. C6.

Solberg, V. S., Howard, K. A., Blustein, D. L., & Close, W. (2002). Career development in the schools: Connecting school-to-work for life. *The Counseling Psychologist, 30*, 705-725.

Steinberg, L. (2004). *The 10 basic principles of good parenting*. New York: Simon and Schuster.

Streeter, L. G. (2004, April 9). Odd man out is not your average boy band. *Palm Beach Post,* pp. E1, E6.

Super, D.E. (1957). *The psychology of careers*. New York: Harper and Row.

Super, D. E. (1963). Self concepts in vocational development. In D. Super, R. Starishevsky, N. Maitlin, & J. Jordan (Eds.), *Career development: Self concept theory* (Monograph 4). New York: CEEB Research.

Super, D. E. (1984). Career and life development. In D. Brown & L. Brooks (Eds.), *Career and choice development* (pp. 192-234). San Francisco: Jossey-Bass.

Taylor, T. (2003). *Family work history*. Livermore, CA: Career Tayloring, Career Counseling & Consulting Services.

Ulrich, D. N., & Dunne, H. P. (1986). *To love and to work: A systematic interlocking of family, workplace, and career.* New York: Brunner Mazel.

Unger, Z. (2004). *Working fire*. New York: Penguin Press.

U. S. Department of Commerce, Bureau of the Census. (1994). *Comparison of income summary measures by selected characteristics, 1-2.* Washington, DC: U.S. Government Printing Office.

Vondracek, F. W., & Kawasaki, T. (1995). Toward a comprehensive framework for adult career development theory and intervention. In B. W. Walsh & S. H.Osipow (Eds.), *Handbook of vocational psychology: Theory, research, and practice* (2nd ed., pp. 111-141). Mahwah, NJ: Erlbaum.

Whiston, S., & Keller, B. (2004). The influences of the family of origin on career development: A review and analysis. *The Counseling Psychologist, 32*, 493-568.

Wilson, J. (2004). *The politics of truth: Inside the lies that led to war and betrayed my wife's CIA identity: A diplomat's memoir.* New York: Carroll and Graf Publishers.

Worthington, R. L., & Juntunen, C. L. (1997). The vocational development of non-college-bound-youth: Counseling psychology and the school-to-work transition movement. *The Counseling Psychologist, 25*, 323-363.

Yalom, I. (1995). *The theory and practice of group psychotherapy* (3rd ed.). New York: Basic Books.

Young, R., & Friesen, J. (1992). The intentions of parents in influencing the career development of their children. *Career Development Quarterly, 40*, 198-207.

Young, R., Friesen, J., & Borycki, B. (1994). Narrative structure and parental influence in career development. *Journal of Adolescence, 17*, 173-191.

Young, R. A., Valach, L., & Collin, A. (1996). A contextual explanation of career. In D. Brown, L. Brooks, & Associates (Eds.), *Career choice and development* (3rd ed., pp. 477-508). San Francisco, CA: Jossey-Bass.

Zedeck, S., & Mosier, K. L. (1990). Work in the family and employing organization. *American Psychologist, 45*, 240-251.